From the Hearth®
Volume 1

by Karen M. Stevens

Illustrated by Patricia A. Riccio

Designed by Jennifer Harper

Layout by Mary Ellen Mulshine and Jessica H...

Recipe Analysis Recipes Computer Analyzed by Micro Cookbook Software, Pinpoint Publishing.

Illustrations by Patricia A. Riccio. For more information regarding the illustrator or to commission work, please contact Karen M. Stevens, From the Hearth@aol.com.

Designed by Jennifer Harper; Layouts by Mary Ellen Mulshine and Jessica Hagenbuch.

Author: Karen M. Stevens, PO Box 2368, Darien, IL 60561 USA
Fax: 630-321-0458
Email: info@Fromthehearth.com

ISBN: 0-9704682-0-2

Introduction

From the Hearth® 1 is a collection of my families (and close friends) Polish, Italian and General recipes. This three book series of recipes has been collected over many years. Often times, I had friends over for dinner and cooked many of these meals. My friends wanted my 'recipes'. Since I learned to cook by watching and tasting while my mother, grandmother's or aunt's prepared meals, I had a challenge ahead of me compiling actual recipes. This series of cookbooks has been over five years in the making.

These recipes are written as dictated or taught to me, using most of the original ingredients. Although you may not wish to cook some of the recipes on a daily basis, just being able to sample the full flavors of old-world cooking will make your mouth water.

However, in our weight and calorie conscious society, recipes in this book may be substituted with low fat alternatives for a more healthy meal. In the section entitled Weights, Measures & Substitutes, you will find emergency or fat reduction substitution guidelines, making these recipes easier to use on a daily basis.

Experiment with the recipes and write your own variations directly in the book for future reference. Note that at the end of each recipe, we have included a section for you to incorporate your own variations or product substitutions.

Enjoy and Mangia Mangia (eat, eat) and enjoy!

Dedication

This cookbook is lovingly dedicated to:

Grandma Lil (whose picture appears on the cover) a primary contributor to my family recipe collection

My Mom Hazel (for cutting me loose in the kitchen over the years)

My Aunt MaryJane (who lovingly supported and guided me over the years)

My sister Pat (a dear friend and talented artist, who drew all of the pictures)

My friends for their support and encouragement over the years helped me realize my dream of publishing this series of cookbooks:

Debbie (without her asking for recipes and working with me on weekends to measure out all ingredients, I may never have written this cookbook)

Barbara (for patience, support and friendship)

Shara Lyn (for spiritual guidance, patience, support and friendship) and to her Family who always stood by and were ready to taste any meals I was willing to conjur up.

Gloria (my lifelong friend and eager contributor of her mom's (my Auntie Delores) and families much loved recipes)

Stuart (my first boss and mentor for always encouraging and teaching me to pursue my dreams)

Greg, Ida, Gregory & Frederic who always were eager samplers and critics

A special and warm thank you go out to many friends and associates over the years who sampled my cooking and encouraged me to write a cookbook.

Most of all to my future husband John and "step-children" Brandan and Becky (and future brother-in-law Bob) who were avid taste-testers and sampled most of the cooking and gave me support and ideas for more recipes for future publication.

In Memory Of...

To beloved family and friends who taught me the joy of cooking, patience and helped shape my life.

Grandma Lil & Grandpa Alex
Nanna Crabb
Aunt Vi
Uncle George
Barbara Locke
Auntie Anna
Jean Minutello-Torio
Auntie Marcella & Uncle Roman
Aunt Helen & Uncle Floyd
Grandpa Joseph & Grandma Catherine
Merlo Bailey

John R. Getz
Best Friend and Love of my Life
We Miss You

Special Notes for My Food Enthusiasts

Please look in the last few pages of this book. There is a form for you to submit your favorite family recipe and a little notation about your memories regarding the dish. If your recipe is selected for an upcoming cookbook, you will receive a free copy of the cookbook and a discount off a future cookbook.

We will be unable to confirm recipes received, however, we will notify you of acceptance and when to expect receipt of the "From the Hearth" World Wide Collection Volume.

Thank you for your support and contribution.

Table of Contents

Table of Contents (continued from previous page)

Weight and Measurement Conversions

2 gal	8 qts	16 pt	32 cups	256 fl oz.	7.59 liters
1 gal	4 qts	8 pt	16 cups	128 fl oz.	3.79 liters
½ gal	2 qts	4 pt	8 cups	64 fl oz.	1.89 liters
¼ gal	1 qts	2 pt	4 cups	32 fl oz.	.95 liters
	½ qt	1 pt	2 cups	16 fl oz.	.47 liters
	¼ qt	½ pt	1 cups	8 fl oz.	.24 liters
1 cup	8 fl oz.	16 tbs	48 tsp	237 ml	
¾ cup	6 fl oz.	12 tbs	36 tsp	177 ml	
⅔ cup	5 fl oz.	10 tbs	32 tsp	158 ml	
½ cup	4 fl oz.	8 tbs	24 tsp	118 ml	
⅓ cup	2 fl oz.	5 tbs	16 tsp	79 ml	
¼ cup	2 fl oz.	4 tbs	12 tsp	59 ml	
⅛ cup	1 fl oz.	2 tbs	6 tsp	30 ml	
	½ fl oz.	1 tbs	3 tsp	15 ml	
		dash	⅛ tsp		

Weights & Measures

Measurements

One Pound Equivalents

2 cups butter

2 cups milk

2⅓ cups dry beans

4 cups all-purpose flour

9 medium eggs

2 cups ground, packed meat

2 cups granulated sugar

2⅔ cups oatmeal or brown sugar

3½ cups sifted powdered sugar

1⅞ cups rice

Can Measurements

Can Size	Weight	Measurement
No 300	14 to 16 oz.	1¾ cups
No 303	16 to 17 oz.	2 cups
No 2	1 lb 4 oz.	2½ cups
No 2½	1 lb 13 oz.	3½ cups
No 10	6½ to 7¼ lbs	12 to 13 cups

Equivalent Pan Sizes

2 8-inch layer pans   or   1½ to 2 dozen cupcakes in muffin tins

3 8-inch layer pans   or   2 9-inch square pans

1 9-inch layer pan   or   1 8-inch square pan

2 9-inch layer pans   or   1 13x9-inch pan   or 1 9-inch tube pan   or   2 8-inch square pans

1 9x5-inch loaf pan   or   2 doz.en cupcakes in muffin tins

Weight of Common Ingredients

Food	Weight of 1 Cup
All-purpose flour, sifted	5 oz.
Butter or solid shortening	8 oz.
Cake flour, sifted	$3\frac{1}{2}$ oz.
Cheese, grated	4 oz.
Eggs, whole	8 oz.
Honey	12 oz.
Milk	8 oz.
Nuts, coarsely chopped	4 oz.
Sugar, granulated	7 oz.
Sugar, light brown, packed	$7\frac{1}{2}$ oz.
Sugar, powdered	4 oz.
Vegetable oil	9 oz.

Common Ingredients & Substitutions

Metric Conversions

1 oz.	28.35 grams (g)
454 g	1 pound (lb.)
2.2 lb.	1 kilogram (kg)
1 tsp.	5 milliliters (ml)
1 Tbsp.	15 ml
1 c.	24 liters (lt) or 250 milliliters
1 gal.	3.8 lt

Temperatures

To convert Fahrenheit into Centigrade, subtract 32 from the temperature, multiply by 5, divide by 9. To convert Centigrade into Fahrenheit, reverse the process: multiply the temperature by 9, divide by 5, add 32.

32 F	freezing point of water	0 C
180 F	simmering point of water	82 C
212 F	boiling point of water	100 C
240 F	soft ball stage for sugar syrup	116 C
260 F	hard ball stage for sugar syrup	127 C
300 F	hard crack stage for sugar syrup	149 C
338 F	sugar caramelizes	170 C
250-275 F	Very low oven	121-133 C
300-325 F	Low oven	149-163 C
350-375 F	Moderate oven	177-190 C
400-425 F	Hot oven	204-218 C
450-475 F	Very hot oven	232-246 C
500-525 F	Extremely hot oven	260-274 C

Emergency Substitutions

1 c. cake flour	1 cup minus 2 Tbp. all-purpose flour
1 cup self rising flour	1 cup all-purpose flour, $\frac{1}{2}$ tsp. baking soda, $1\frac{1}{2}$ tsp baking powder and $\frac{1}{2}$ tsp salt
1 Tbp. cornstarch (for thickening)	2 Tbp. all-purpose flour
1 tsp. baking powder	$\frac{1}{2}$ tsp. cream of tarter + $\frac{1}{4}$ tsp. baking soda OR $\frac{1}{4}$ tsp. baking soda + $\frac{1}{2}$ cup buttermilk or sour milk (which will replace $\frac{1}{2}$ cup liquid in recipe)
1 package active dry yeast	1 cake compressed yeast
1 package active dry yeast	1 cake compressed yeast or $2\frac{1}{4}$ tsp. yeast
1 c. sugar	1 c. packed brown sugar or 2 c. powdered sugar
1 c. honey	$1\frac{1}{4}$ c. sugar plus $\frac{1}{4}$ c. liquid
1 c. corn syrup	1 c. sugar plus $\frac{1}{4}$ c. liquid
1 c. light cream	1 Tbs. melted butter plus enough milk to make 1 c.
1 c. milk	$\frac{1}{2}$ cup evaporated milk + $\frac{1}{2}$ cup water
1 cup sweet condensed milk	$\frac{7}{8}$ cup Non-dairy creamer + $\frac{1}{4}$ cup sugar
1 cup whole milk	$\frac{1}{2}$ cup non-dairy creamer + $\frac{1}{2}$ cup water
1 cup skim milk	$\frac{1}{4}$ cup non-dairy cream + $\frac{3}{4}$ cup water
1 cup sour cream	16 oz. non-fat cottage cheese + 2 Tbs. non-fat yogurt + 1 or 2 Tbs. lemon juice

1 egg	$\frac{1}{4}$ cup egg substitute (such as Egg Beater)
1 egg	2 egg whites (beaten until fluffy, then add to recipe)
2 cups tomato sauce	$\frac{3}{4}$ cup tomato paste plus 1 cup water
1 clove garlic	$\frac{1}{8}$ tsp. garlic powder OR $\frac{1}{8}$ tsp. minced dried garlic OR $\frac{1}{2}$ tsp. minced garlic in a jar
1 small onion	1 tsp. onion powder OR 1 Tbs. minced dried onion, rehydrated
1 tsp. dry mustard	1 Tbs. prepared mustard
1 tsp. grated lemon peel	$\frac{1}{2}$ tsp. lemon extract

Crumbs

½ cup bread crumbs — 1 slice dried and grated bread

1 cup graham cracker crumbs — 14 graham cracker squares finely chopped

1 cup chocolate wafers — 18 chocolate wafers finely chopped

1 cup vanilla wafers — 22 vanilla wafers finely chopped

Cheese & Butter

4 oz. cheese — 1 cup shredded

1 lb. cheese — 4 cups shredded

1 stick butter — ½ cup butter

4 sticks butter — 2 cups = 1 lb.

Sugar

1 lb. granulated sugar — 2 cups granulated sugar

1 lb. brown sugar — 2¼ cup brown sugar, packed

1 lb. confectioners' sugar — 3¾ cup confectioners' sugar

Pasta & Rice

Macaroni — 1 cup uncooked = 2½ cups cooked

Noodles — 1 cup uncooked = 2 cups cooked

Spaghetti — 8 oz. uncooked = 4 cups cooked

Rice — 1 cup uncooked = 3 cups cooked

Herbs

1 tsp. dried = 1 Tbs. fresh

Popcorn

¼ cup unpopped = 5 cups popped

Conversions

1 cup white sugar	12 packets Sweet 'N Low packets (or 4 tsp Sweet 'N Low Bulk)
1 cup brown sugar	4 tsp Sweet 'N Low Brown (Bulk)
1 stick butter	½ cup liquid Butter Buds
1 cup oil	1 cup Liquid Butter Buds
1 cup sour cream	16 oz. non-fat cottage cheese + 2 Tbs. non-fat yogurt + 1 or 2 Tbs. lemon juice
1 egg	¼ cup egg substitute (such as Egg Beater)
1 egg	2 egg whites (beaten until fluffy, then add to recipe)
1 cup light cream	1 Tbs. Liquid Butter Buds plus enough skim milk to make 1 cup
1 cup milk	1 cup skim milk OR ½ cup evaporated milk + ½ cup water
1 cup whipped cream	1 cup Dream Whip prepared as instructed

Allspice, Sweet. Great with fruits, desserts, beef, pork, ham and tomato sauces

Basil: eggs, mushrooms, pasta, salads, tomatoes

Bay Leaf: fish, game, marinades, poultry, soup, stews

Chives: Cream cheese, herb butter, mayonnaise, omelettes, salads, soup

Cinnamon, Sweet. Great with desserts, fruits, tomato sauces, pork, chicken

Cloves, Sweet and aromatic. Desserts, baked goods, lamb, pork

Comfrey: pickles, salads, wine

Coriander: Cauliflower, celery, curries, fish, pickled fruit

Dill: Cheese, eggs, pickles, salads, soup, white sauces

Garlic: Beef, Italian dishes, pork, lamb, salad dressings, stews, vegetables

Ginger, Sweet. Fruits, baked goods, squash

Oregano: Tomato sauces, chicken, lamb, stews, vegetables

Parsley: Bouquet garni, fish, salads, soup, stews, vegetables

Rosemary: Beef, chicken, lamb, pork, tomatoes

Sage: Beef, lamb, mutton, salads, sausages, soup, veal

Tarragon: Bernaise & tartar sauces, chicken, eggs, fish, salads, tomatoes

Age - Often done with meat products and cheeses to improve their flavor. These foods are stored in a temperature controlled environment for specific time periods.

Bake - A dry heat cooking method that uses the oven. When meats are cooked this way it is called roasting.

Barbecue - A low fat method of cooking using direct heat on an outdoor grill. Also food cooked in a spicy sauce over a grill.

Baste - To moisten food with liquid,wine,marinade or drippings to prevent it from drying out or burning and to add flavor.

Beat - To mix rapidly with a spoon, whisk or electric beater using an over and over or round and round motion.

Bind - To stir a thickener, such as egg or flour, into a mixture to make it hold together.

Blanch - To immerse quickly in boiling water to loosen skins, or to help set color and flavor, especially important for preparing vegetables for freezing.

Boil - To cook liquid until bubbles break the surface, at 212 degrees fahrenheit for water at sea level.

Braise - To brown in small amount of fat or nonstick cooking spray; then a small amount of liquid is added and the food is covered and slowly oven baked or simmered on a stove top.

Broil - To cook under direct heat. Foods must be turned and watched closely to prevent burning. Broil meats on a rack to let the fat drip off.

Brown - To cook food until it turns brown, either on top of the stove in a pan with a little fat or nonstick cooking spray, in the oven or under a broiler.

Glossary of Cooking Terms

Caramelize - To heat sugar until it has browned or to coat food with caramelized sugar.

Clarify - To clear cloudy liquid, usually by heating with raw egg white, then straining through cloth. Butter may also be clarified by melting it slowly over heat. The milk solids sink to the bottom, leaving clear, yellow butter that does not burn as quickly.

Chop - To cut food into small pieces by hand or with a chopper. Larger than mince.

Cream - To mix an ingredient or ingredients, usually fat and something else, until creamy.

Crimp - To seal the edge of a pie or pastry in a decorative manner.

Cube - To cut into uniform cube shape, equal measure on all sides.

Cure - To preserve meat, fish or cheese by salting, drying and/or smoking.

Cut in - To mix shortening or other fat with dry ingredients until the mixture is coarse and crumbly.

Deglaze - To scrape the browned bits off the bottom of a cooking pan by adding liquid and heating gently. This is added to a dish for flavor.

Devein - To remove the black vein along the top of shrimp.

Dice - To cut food into small cubes or squares, usually $\frac{1}{8}$ to $\frac{1}{4}$ inch; smaller than cubes.

Dilute - To weaken or thin by adding liquid.

Dissolve - To mix a dry ingredient with liquid until it becomes part of the liquid solution.

Dredge - To coat food with flour, cornmeal, bread crumbs, sugar or other dry ingredient.

Eviscerate - To remove the entrails from animal foods.

Fillet - A boneless piece of meat or fish, or the process of deboning the meat or fish.

Flute - To make a decorative edge on pies or pastries; to crimp.

Fold - To blend two mixtures using a spoon or spatula with a motion that brings food from the bottom up and over the ingredients.

Fricassee - A method of braising cut-up chicken or small game in which the pieces are dredged and browned, then cooked, covered in liquid, often with vegetables. This can be done on the stove top or in the oven.

Fry - To cook food in hot fat, usually in a pan on the stove. The food can be totally immersed or in part way.

Grease - To lightly coat a surface with oil, butter or nonstick cooking spray.

Grill - To cook under or over direct heat, usually charcoal or hardwood.

Hull - To remove the outer covering of a berry or seed, as in removing the green tops from strawberries.

Husk - To remove the coarse outer covering, as in corn, or the outer covering itself.

Julienne - To cut foods, usually vegetables, into small match like strips.

Knead - To repeatedly fold, press and work dough with the hands on a smooth surface until it is a cohesive mass.

Glossary of Cooking Terms

Macerate - To soak fruit in a spirit mixture.

Marinate - To steep foods in a spicy liquid for several hours, allowing the mixture time to absorb the flavors. Sometimes it is used for tenderizing, too.

Mince - To cut into fine pieces. More finely cut than chopped.

Mull - To heat fruit juice, wine, ale or other alcoholic beverage with sugar and spices.

Pan-broil - To cook in an uncovered skillet over direct heat with as little fat as possible. Fat is poured off as it accumulates.

Pan-fry - To cook in a skillet with some fat without pouring off drippings.

Parboil - To boil food until partially cooked and complete cooking with some other method.

Pare - To cut the peelings from fruit or vegetables with a peeler or sharp knife.

Pickle - To preserve in brine or vinegar.

Pipe - To apply a frilly border by pushing the substance, usually frosting, mashed potatoes or pureed vegetables, through a pastry bag with a decorative tip.

Poach - To simmer food gently in hot liquid.

Proof - To set a yeast mixture in a warm spot to rise.

Puree - To make food into a smooth mixture by pressing through a sieve or food mill, or whirling in a food processor or blender.

Reconstitute - to restore dehydrated food to a liquid state by adding water.

Reduce - To evaporate by boiling to reduce volume and concentrate flavors.

Refresh - To plunge hot food, usually vegetables, into ice water to set the color and flavor.

Render - To melt solid fat, usually animal fat, by cooking slowly.

Roast - To cook uncovered in the oven by dry heat or over a spit.

Saute - To cook food over direct heat with a little fat in a skillet or small pan.

Scald - To heat liquid to the point just before it boils. For milk, this is when bubbles begin to gather around the edge of the pan.

Scallop - To bake in cream or a cream sauce or layers of foods baked in a casserole beneath a layer of bread crumb topping. Also, thinly sliced rounds or meat such as veal or lobster.

Score - To make shallow knife cuts over the surface of a food, usually in a criss-cross pattern. Usually done for the fat of roast or ham.

Sear - To brown meat quickly, either in a very hot oven or in a skillet over high heat, to seal in the juices.

Separate - To remove one part from another, as in separating the egg whites from the yolks.

Sieve - To strain liquid through a strainer; also the name for the strainer.

Sift - To put dry ingredients through a sieve or sifter.

Simmer - To heat liquid to about 185 degrees fahrenheit, just until bubbles begin to form, just below the boiling point. Also cooking food in simmering liquid.

Sliver - To cut food into thin shreds.

Glossary of Cooking Terms

Glossary of Cooking Terms

Snip - To cut into fine pieces with scissor or knife; works especially well with fresh herbs.

Spit-roast - To cook on a spit, usually outdoors over a open flame.

Steam - To cook food by direct steam by placing it on a rack placed in a container with boiling water. Steam cooks faster than boiling and preserves more nutrients.

Steep - To let a substance, such as tea or coffee grounds, stand in hot liquid until their flavor is extracted.

Stir-fry - The Oriental method of quickly cooking food, usually in a wok, using very little oil.

Stud - To insert whole cloves, slivers of garlic or other seasoning into the surface of food.

Stuff - To fill with stuffing.

Temper - To lower the temperature to provide the correct consistency, applies to chocolate.

Truss - To secure legs and wings of poultry or game with string so that it will cook more evenly.

Turn - To flute or scallop food, especially baby vegetables and mushrooms. Also, to turn food over as it cooks.

Whip - To beat mixture by hand or with electric mixer, incorporating air and increasing the volume. Usually done to cream or egg whites.

Whisk - A wire implement used for beating.

Zest - The colored part of the citrus rind used as flavoring; a tool called a zester is used to remove citrus zest.

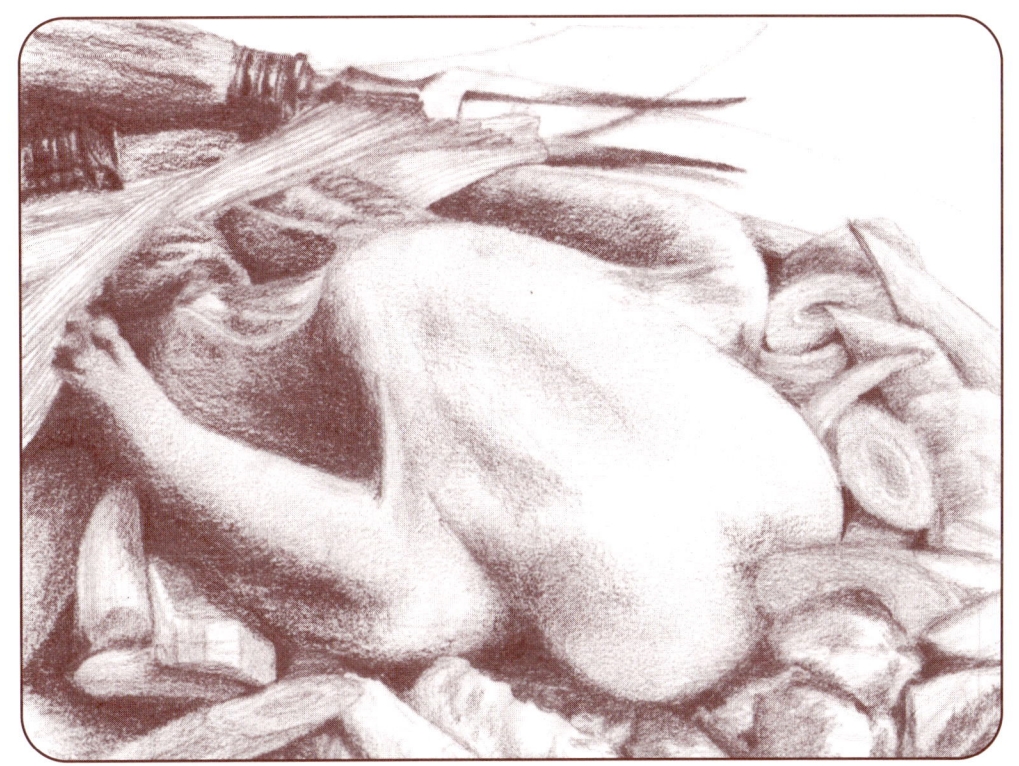

Chicken

Breaded Chicken

Serves   6

Preparation   :10   Cook   :30   Stand   :00   Total   :40

This same recipe can be used for veal or pork.

Ingredients

4	boneless chicken breasts, cut in half
1 to 2	eggs, slightly beaten
1 to 1½	cups bread crumbs, (you may use Italian seasoned crumbs, then omit following items)
1	teaspoon garlic powder
1	tablespoon parsley flakes, dried
3 to 4	tablespoons Romano cheese, grated
2 to 4	tablespoons cannola oil
½ to ¾	cup arrowroot

Source: Auntie Mary Jane Stevens

Beat egg(s) and place in bowl for dipping. In a separate bowl add bread crumbs, garlic powder, parsley and cheese. Mix well.

Using a large skillet (preferably a cast iron skillet), heat 2-4 tablespoons of cannola oil or light olive oil. Dip chicken in eggs, then into bread crumb mixture. Place in well heated skillet for 1-2 minutes. Turn over and cook for another 1-2 minutes. Remove from skillet and place on a baking sheet. Cook in a preheated 325 degree oven for approximately 20 minutes, until chicken is done.

If you prefer, you can cook the chicken entirely in the skillet, just let it properly brown and cook on the stove top for 6-8 minutes, until chicken is done. (More or less time may be needed, depending on how thick the chicken, veal or pork is cooked).

Nutrition (per serving): 266 calories

Saturated Fat	2g	
Total Fat	8g	(27% of calories)
Protein	38g	(58% of calories)
Carbohydrates	10g	(15% of calories)
Cholesterol	129mg	
Sodium	145mg	

My Notes and Recipe Variations

Chicken

Chicken and Prosciutto

Serves 4-6

Preparation :30 Cook :45 Stand :00 Total 1:15

Ingredients

4	chicken breasts
1	cup mozzarella cheese, shredded or grated
8	slices Prosciutto, sliced very thin
4	fresh garlic cloves, diced
½	cup bread crumbs
1	egg
2	teaspoons Romano cheese
¼	cup Italian flat-leaf parsley, finely chopped

salt and pepper, to taste

Using a meat tenderizer, pound chicken to tenderize and make about ⅛ inch thick. Lightly brush a little olive oil over chicken. In a small bowl, add bread crumbs, egg, parsley, Romano cheese, salt and pepper. Mix well. Sprinkle mozzarella cheese over meat. Use ¼ of stuffing (bread crumb mixture) and spread over cheese. Add 2 slices of Prosciutto over mixture. Roll chicken and tie with string or thread to ensure nothing falls from roll.

In a skillet, add a little oil and lightly brown chicken. Sprinkle with a little extra parsley. Bake in a 350 degree oven for 45 minutes to 1 hour.

Since oven temperatures vary, check after 30 and 45 minutes so meat will not overcook.

Nutrition (per serving): 375 calories

Saturated Fat	6g
Total Fat	13g (28% of calories)
Protein	74 g (70% of calories)
Carbohydrates	3g (2% of calories)
Cholesterol	230mg
Sodium	1021 mg

My Notes and Recipe variations

Chicken

Chicken and Rice Florentine

Serves   4

Preparation   :15   Cook   :40   Stand   :00   Total   :55

Great fix ahead meal for hectic weekends or evenings. Will keep for 2-3 days in the refrigerator. This is also a great recipe to use with leftover rice and baked or broiled chicken.

Ingredients

1	cup raw rice
4	cups chicken broth (low salt)
2	10 oz. packages frozen spinach, thawed and drained
4	chicken breasts, (or veal cutlets)
3	tablespoons butter
3	tablespoons flour
⅓	cup dry white wine, (Madieri)

Use a 4-5 quart Dutch oven. Place 2 cups of broth and rice in the pot and bring to a boil. Reduce heat and simmer until cooked.

Place cooked rice in the bottom of a 13x9 lightly oiled baking dish (or spray with non-stick vegetable spray). Using same pan, add 2 tablespoons oil and heat. Place in chicken breasts and cook on all sides until lightly browned (3-4 minutes each side). Place chicken over rice.

Using same pan, melt the butter and stir in flour until smooth. Add remaining broth and wine. Mix well. Add spinach, cook until well heated. Spoon mixture over chicken and spread evenly.

Bake in a 350 degree oven for 20-25 minutes. If pre-making, the cooking time in the oven will need to be slightly longer to ensure the cold food is well heated.

Nutrition (per serving): 646 calories

Saturated Fat	7g
Total Fat	14g (19% of calories)
Protein	65g (41% of calories)
Carbohydrates	62g (39% of calories)
Cholesterol	160mg
Sodium	807mg

My Notes and Recipe Variations

Chicken

Chicken Cacciatore

Serves   6

Preparation   :10   Cook   :45   Stand   :00   Total   :55

Ingredients

1	whole chicken, cut up
1	14 oz. can pitted black olives
1½	cups dry red wine
1	12 ounce tomato sauce
1	12 oz. can water
2	fresh garlic cloves, diced
1	teaspoon oregano
1	teaspoon salt
1	teaspoon black pepper
2	tablespoons extra light olive oil

In a large skillet or dutch oven, add olive oil. Saute garlic until tender. Add chicken pieces and brown on all sides. Add wine, tomato sauce and water. Mix well. Reduce heat to simmer and cover.

Continue cooking chicken until done and tender (about ½ hour). Check after 15 minutes to ensure sauce is thickening, but not evaporated. (Cook an additional 15 minutes). Drain black olives. Add the olives 5 minutes before you finish cooking the chicken. The dish is done when chicken starts pulling from bone.

Suggestion:

Cut 4-6 red potatoes in bite sized pieces and add to pot with chicken 15 minutes after you add wine and sauce to chicken. Or serve with a side of pasta and tomato sauce.

Nutrition (per serving): 513 calories

Saturated Fat	9g	
Total Fat	38g	(66% of calories)
Protein	34g	(26% of calories)
Carbohydrates	10g	(8% of calories)
Cholesterol	157mg	
Sodium	1437mg	

My Notes and Recipe Variations

Chicken

Chicken Fra Diavlo (Spicy chicken in tomato sauce)

Serves 4

Preparation :20 Cook :30 Stand :00 Total :50

Ingredients

4	boneless chicken breasts, cut into 1 inch slices
2	tablespoons extra light olive oil
1	medium sweet onion, chopped or cut into strips
1	small green bell pepper, cleaned and cut into strips
1	small red bell pepper, cleaned and cut into strips
1	small yellow bell pepper, cleaned and cut into strips
1½	cups chicken stock, (or 1 can chicken broth)
1	16 oz. can crushed tomato
1	teaspoon bottled hot pepper sauce
2 to 4	Italian peppers, spicy and hot, diced or chopped
2	fresh garlic cloves, diced to taste salt
4 to 6	canned stewed tomatoes, (or fresh tomatoes peeled and chopped)
½	cup unbleached flour, (add salt and pepper to taste)
12	spinach leaves, cut in half, Optional

Dredge chicken in flour and coat well. Add 2 tablespoons oil to skillet and brown chicken on all sides. Remove chicken from skillet.

Add 2 tablespoons oil to skillet and saute the onions, peppers and garlic, until tender crisp. Add remaining ingredients (except chicken). Bring to a boil, then reduce heat to simmer. Mix well and cook an additional 20 minutes. Place chicken on top of vegetable mixture. Remove from heat and cover for 10 minutes. Serve hot.

You can also serve with a small side of pasta.

Nutrition (per serving): 477 calories

Saturated Fat	2g	
Total Fat	11g	(20% of calories)
Protein	60g	(50% of calories)
Carbohydrates	35g	(29% of calories)
Cholesterol	137mg	
Sodium	826mg	

My Notes and Recipe variations

Chicken

Chicken in Wine Sauce

Serves 6

Preparation :25 Cook 2:00 Stand :00 Total 2:25

This recipe can also be used for veal shanks and served with a Mushroom Risotto (Arborio Rice)

Ingredients

4	chicken breasts, (or 1 to $\frac{1}{2}$ inch thick veal shanks)
2	cups dry white wine
8 to 10	boiling onions, (small), optional
$1\frac{1}{2}$	cups mushrooms, sliced
1	teaspoon basil
4 to 6	fresh garlic cloves, smashed or sliced
16 to 20	baby carrots, fresh
2 to 3	tablespoons extra light olive oil
$\frac{1}{4}$ to $\frac{1}{2}$	cup unbleached flour, to dredge chicken in
2	tablespoons flour, cornstarch or arrowroot (I sometimes mix equal amounts of each)
$\frac{1}{2}$	cup cold water

In a large Dutch oven, add olive oil and heat. Add garlic and saute until tender. Remove garlic from pan. Place chicken (or veal) in a plastic bag with the flour, salt and paprika. Seal well and shake, dredging chicken or veal fully.

Add oil to dutch oven, heat. Remove chicken or veal from bag and place in Dutch oven and brown on all sides. Add wine and mushrooms to the pan and bring to a boil. Reduce heat to simmer. Add cleaned and peeled (but whole) boiling onions. Cover pot and let cook until meat is tender $1\frac{1}{2}$ to 2 hours. (For veal, you may need to cook longer so veal starts coming off bone.) Remove meat and onions from wine broth.

Add 1 to 2 cups of chicken stock (or 1 can chicken broth with 1 can water; 15 oz size) to the wine broth in Dutch oven; add the baby carrots. Bring to a boil and reduce heat. Continue cooking until carrots are tender. Using a small jar, add 2 tablespoons of cornstarch or flour with $\frac{1}{4}$ to $\frac{1}{2}$ cup cold water. Shake well until smooth. Slowly pour flour or cornstarch mixture into liquid in the Dutch oven. Stirring constantly until slightly thickened. Place Meat and onions back in pot and cook for an additional 5-10 minutes. Serve with Mushroom Risotto or serve over rice.

Nutrition (per serving): 520 calories

Saturated Fat	2g
Total Fat	11g (12% of calories)
Protein	64g (32% of calories)
Carbohydrates	73g (36% of calories)
Cholesterol	137mg
Sodium	213mg

My Notes and Recipe Variations

Chicken

Chicken Italiano

Serves   6

Preparation   :15   Cook   :30   Stand   :00   Total   :45

Ingredients

2	boneless chicken breasts, whole
1	teaspoon salt
2	teaspoons garlic powder
1	teaspoon pepper
3	tablespoons light olive oil
2	cups spaghetti sauce
1	teaspoon oregano
2	cups celery, sliced
3	cups cooked rice

Sprinkle salt, pepper, and garlic powder over chicken. In large Dutch oven add oil and heat. Add chicken and saute for 2 minutes on each side.

Stir in spaghetti sauce and remaining seasonings. Cover and simmer for 10-15 minutes. Add celery and continue cooking until celery is tender crisp. Serve over bed of rice or pasta. Sprinkle with Romano cheese, if desired.

Nutrition (per serving): 349 calories

Saturated Fat	2g
Total Fat	11g (28% of calories)
Protein	22g (26% of calories)
Carbohydrates	40g (46% of calories)
Cholesterol	46mg
*Sodium	1000mg

*To reduce sodium content, use homemade spaghetti sauce and eliminate salt, or use reduced salt sauce.

My Notes and Recipe Variations

Chicken

Chicken Mediterranean

Serves   6

Preparation   :20   Cook   :25   Stand   1:00   Total   1:45

This dish is terrific served over cappelini.

Ingredients

4	chicken breasts
1	teaspoon oregano
2	7-inch long zucchinis
1	7-inch long yellow squash
1	cup broccoli florets, diced
1	carrot, diced
1	cup dry white wine
2	teaspoons balsamic vinegar
2	scallions including tops, chopped
2	fresh garlic cloves, diced
8 to 10	Italian tomatoes, peeled and cut into quarters (or stewed Italian tomatoes)
1	pound pasta
2	tablespoons extra virgin olive oil
2	teaspoons fresh basil, chopped
1	tablespoon Italian flat-leaf parsley, chopped

Cut chicken into bite sized cubes (or strips). Place in freezer bag or plastic container. Add wine, vinegar, garlic, salt and pepper. Mix well. Set in refrigerator and marinade for 1 hour.

Fill pot with water to cook pasta as directed. While water is heating prepare balance of recipe.

In skillet, add olive oil. Heat. Add chicken. Reserve the marinade. Saute for 3 minutes, turning constantly. Add remaining ingredients (EXCEPT tomatoes) and saute an additional 2-3 minutes. Add marinade and tomatoes. Simmer over low to medium heat for 10-15 minutes; when vegetables are tender. Toss over cappelini.

Nutrition (per serving): 514 calories

Saturated Fat	1g
Total Fat	9g (16% of calories)
Protein	48g (37% of calories)
Carbohydrates	54g (42% of calories)
Cholesterol	146mg
Sodium	150mg

My Notes and Recipe variations

Chicken

Serves   4

Preparation   :20   Cook   :20   Stand   :00   Total   :40

Ingredients

4	spilt chicken breasts, (or veal)
2	tablespoons extra virgin olive oil
½	cup dry white wine
¼	cup lemon juice
1	teaspoon salt
1	teaspoon coarsely ground black pepper
1	tablespoon Italian flat-leaf parsley, chopped
1	cup fresh mushrooms, sliced
1	egg
½	cup flour, (to lightly bread chicken)

Using a meat tenderizer or mallet, pound the chicken breasts (or veal) to about $\frac{1}{8}$ inch.

Beat egg in bowl with 1 tablespoon water. Dip 1 chicken breast in egg. Drain slightly. Place flour (about fi cup, salt and pepper) in a plastic bag. Add chicken breasts and shake until well coated.

In a skillet (preferably a cast iron skillet, place 2 tablespoons olive oil and heat. Add chicken and cook over low heat until lightly browned, then turn and cook other size (about 3 minutes on each side). Cook all chicken breasts in this manner, adding more oil as needed. Remove chicken from skillet and place on a plate (keep warm in a 175-200 degree oven).

Saute garlic (and scallions) in the same pan until tender. Pour wine and lemon juice into the pan and bring to a boil. Scrape pan to dislodge flour bits. Boil sauce for several minutes. Reduce to simmer and add sliced mushrooms (optional) and parsley. Cook for 5 minutes. Pour the sauce over chicken breasts and serve.

Nutrition (per serving): 357 calories

Saturated Fat	2g
Total Fat	11g (28% of calories)
Protein	57g (63% of calories)
Carbohydrates	3g (3% of calories)
Cholesterol	190mg
Sodium	759mg

My Notes and Recipe Variations

Chicken

Chicken Paprika

Serves   4

Preparation :15   Cook :30   Stand :00   Total :45

Chicken dish takes great served over linguine or white rice.

Ingredients

1	pound boneless chicken, cut into bite sized pieces
½	cup chicken broth
2½	teaspoons unbleached flour
1½	teaspoons paprika, add more depending on flavor desired
½	teaspoon salt
1	diced medium sweet onion
3	garlic cloves, minced
5	tablespoons sour cream
½	cup water
¼	cup extra virgin olive oil, for sauteing chicken, and onion

garlic
fresh parsley, snipped, for garnish

In a jar or container with lid, add ½ cup cold water, paprika and 1½ teaspoons flour. Shake well until fully blended. In a large pot, add chicken broth, water and flour mixture; stir well. Set aside.

In a large skillet, spray with spray vegetable oil and saute onions and garlic; cook until tender. Add chicken pieces; spray about 3-4 seconds of vegetable spray over chicken, stir and cook until chicken is lightly browned. Add flour and paprika mixture.

Stirring well. Cook until mixture begins to boil, stirring often. Reduce heat to low; cover and simmer 20-25 minutes. Remove from heat and stir in sour cream. Sprinkle with parsley (optional). Serve over pasta or rice.

Cook 1 pound of pasta or enough for 3 cups rice.

Nutrition (per serving): 439 calories

Saturated Fat	8g	
Total Fat	35g	(71% of calories)
Protein	23g	(21% of calories)
Carbohydrates	9g	(8% of calories)
Cholesterol	109mg	
Sodium	566mg	

My Notes and Recipe Variations

Chicken

Chicken Parmigiana

Serves   6

Preparation   :15   Cook   1:00   Stand   :00   Total   1:15

Ingredients

2 to 3	cups of —SPAGHETTI SAUCE—MEATLESS
4	chicken breasts, sliced thinly ($\frac{1}{4}$ inch thick)
1	cup mozzarella cheese, grated
$\frac{1}{4}$	cup Romano cheese
1	cup unbleached flour
1	egg, well beaten
1	teaspoon water
2	tablespoons olive oil
1	teaspoon salt
1	teaspoon black pepper
$\frac{1}{2}$	cup Romano cheese, grated

Partially freeze chicken breasts so they will be easier to slice. Cut each chicken breast into $\frac{1}{4}$ inch thick. Using a meat tenderizer, pound the chicken to tenderize and further flatten.

In a large bowl, add flour, salt, pepper. In a separate bowl, beat egg with 1 tablespoon of water. Heat a skillet and place 2 tablespoons olive oil in skillet. Dip the chicken into the egg mixture, then the flour mixture; coating well. Place in heated skillet and cook over medium heat until lightly browned on all sides. Remove chicken from skillet and place on paper towel to remove excess oil.

Use a baking dish of 9x12x3. Place a small amount of spaghetti sauce in bottom of dish. Carefully line the bottom with breaded chicken. Add sauce on top of chicken and sprinkle mozzarella cheese, add the remaining sauce and chicken on top. Bake in a 350 degree oven for 30-45 minutes, until chicken is tender. Bon Appetito!

Nutrition (per serving): 392 calories

Saturated Fat	6g	
Total Fat	15g	(34% of calories)
Protein	47g	(48% of calories)
Carbohydrates	18g	(19% of calories)
Cholesterol	152mg	
Sodium	724mg	

My Notes and Recipe Variations

Chicken

Chicken Pomodoro

Serves   4

Preparation   :25   Cook   1:00   Stand   :00   Total   1:25

This recipe can be made with or without the stuffing by using sliced tomatoes, and following the Bracioli recipe.

Ingredients

4	split chicken breasts
1	cup mozzarella cheese, shredded, grated
1	small red pepper, finely chopped
2	tablespoons Romano cheese, grated
1	egg
2	tomatoes, diced
1	teaspoon oregano
2	tablespoons Italian flat-leaf parsley, finely chopped
1	cup bread crumbs
1	teaspoon paprika, used for all roll ups
4	fresh garlic cloves, chopped
2	tablespoons water
1	teaspoon lemon juice

Using a meat tenderizer or mallet, pound the chicken until $1/8$ inch thick. Lightly brush the chicken with olive oil. In a mixing bowl add remaining ingredients and mix well.

Separate stuffing into 4 sections and spread stuffing over chicken. Spread evenly. Roll chicken lengthwise and tie with string or thread to secure all ends.

In a lightly greased skillet, brown chicken until light brown. Place in a baking dish and bake in a 350 degree oven for 45 minutes to 1 hour. Since oven temperatures vary, check meat after 30 minutes and 45 minutes to determine if done.

Variation:

As an alternative, omit the bread crumbs and egg and slice the tomatoes thin to medium thin. Lightly saute in an ungreased skillet the tomatoes to remove extra juice. Place tomatoes on chicken, side by side, add mozzarella and spread evenly. Shake Romano cheese, oregano and salt and pepper, to taste. Add parsley and roll as directed above.

Nutrition (per serving): 478 calories

Saturated Fat	6g
Total Fat	12g (23% of calories)
Protein	67g (56% of calories)
Carbohydrates	25g (21% of calories)
Cholesterol	216mg
Sodium	496mg

My Notes and Recipe variations

Chicken

Chicken Wings-Hot and Spicy

Serves   6

Preparation   :20   Cook   1:10   Stand   :00   Total   1:30

Ingredients

24	chicken wings
1	teaspoon salt
1	teaspoon pepper
4	fresh garlic cloves, minced (2-3 teaspoons)
2	tablespoons paprika
$2/3$	cup tarragon wine vinegar, (or balsamic)
$1/3$	cup bottled hot pepper sauce, (or Tabasco)
$1/2$	cup unbleached flour, (more may be used if needed)
$1/4$	cup oil
1	teaspoon cayenne pepper

Clean chicken wings and tuck small end under drumstick end to secure. Place flour, salt, pepper and 1 tablespoon. paprika in a plastic or paper bag. Add chicken and shake well. In a large skillet, add oil and heat. Add chicken wings and lightly brown on all sides. Remove from oil and place on a large cookie sheet or roasting pan.

In a blender, add garlic, paprika, vinegar, hot pepper sauce and 1 tablespoon of the flour mixture. Blend on high to mix well.

Pour over chicken and stir gently to coat. Bake in a 350 to 375 degree oven for 1 hour or until chicken is well cooked. Serve with a chunky blue cheese dressing, Garlic Ranch and celery sticks.

Nutrition (per serving): 468 calories

Saturated Fat	9g	
Total Fat	41g	(65% of calories)
Protein	38g	(27% of calories)
Carbohydrates	12g	(9% of calories)
Cholesterol	151mg	
Sodium	546mg	

My Notes and Recipe Variations

_____
_____
_____
_____
_____
_____
_____
_____
_____
_____
_____
_____
_____
_____
_____
_____
_____

Chicken

Chicken with Garlic

Serves   4

Preparation :20 Cook 1:10 Stand :30 Total 2:00

Ingredients

4	chicken breasts, deboned, with or without skin
2	tablespoons light olive oil
1	teaspoon salt
½	teaspoon black pepper
1	cup chicken broth
2	tablespoons lemon juice, (or tarragon vinegar)
6	tablespoons flour
1	teaspoon paprika
4 to 6	garlic cloves, crushed.

Preheat oven to 375 degrees.

Place the chicken broth, lemon juice (or vinegar) and crushed garlic in an air tight container and cover. Let stand for at least 30 minutes.

Mix the flour, salt, pepper and paprika in a large bowl. In a large skillet add the oil and heat. Place the chicken breasts (one at a time) in the flour and coat heavily. Cook the chicken in the hot oil over a moderate heat until browned on all sides. Place chicken in a baking dish. Continue with all chicken until browned (add more oil if needed).

Pour the chicken broth, lemon juice (or vinegar), and garlic mixture over the chicken. Bake covered for about 1 hour; basting occasionally.

Nutrition (per serving): 472 calories

Saturated Fat	2g	
Total Fat	10g	(20% of calories)
Protein	60g	(50% of calories)
Carbohydrates	35g	(30% of calories)
Cholesterol	137mg	
Sodium	1107mg	

My Notes and Recipe Variations

Chicken

Chicken with Onions and Peppers

Serves 4

Preparation :10   Cook :45   Stand :00   Total :55

Ingredients

2 to 3	green bell peppers, cleaned and cut into 1 inch strips
1	medium sweet onion, cut into strips
2	fresh garlic cloves
3	tablespoons olive oil
1	10 oz. can tomato sauce
½	teaspoon oregano, Optional
1 to 2	bay leaves
½	cup unbleached flour, (or arrowroot)

salt and pepper, to taste

Dredge chicken in flour or arrowroot. Using a large skillet (preferably cast iron), place olive oil and heat. Saute garlic in olive oil until tender. Place chicken into hot oil and lightly brown on both sides. Remove from heat and place on paper towel to remove excess oil. Place tomato sauce and 1 to 1½ cups of water in skillet.

Stir well to loosen browned pieces from pan. Add oregano (if desired), bay leafs, salt and pepper, and peppers and onions. Cook over medium heat for 10 minutes, until flavors blend well.

Using a rectangular baking dish (9x12), place ⅓ of sauce in bottom of baking dish. Arrange chicken, in one layer, over sauce. Pour remaining sauce and peppers and onion mixture over chicken.

Bake covered in a 350 degree oven for approximately 30-45 minutes, until chicken is very tender. Serve with vegetables or over rice or noodles.

Nutrition (per serving): 214 calories

Saturated Fat	1g
Total Fat	11g (45% of calories)
Protein	4g (7% of calories)
Carbohydrates	26g (48% of calories)
Cholesterol	0mg
Sodium	529mg

My Notes and Recipe Variations

Chicken

Chicken with Oregano

Serves   8

Preparation   :10   Cook   1:00   Stand   :00   Total   1:10

Served with roasted or grilled zucchini and yellow squash this makes a taste tempting treat.

Ingredients

1	whole chicken, quartered
1	tablespoon lemon juice
1	tablespoon fresh oregano, chopped
½	cup olive oil
6	fresh garlic cloves, chopped
½	cup dry white wine, if not using wine, increase lemon juice to ½ cup, Optional
1	tablespoon Italian flat-leaf parsley, chopped

For those that love the flavor of oregano, you may wish to add more oregano and reduce the amount of parsley. Place all ingredients in a freezer bag (or air tight container). Shake well to ensure chicken is well coated. Marinade for 1 hour. Place chicken in a baking dish, with all of the marinade. Salt and pepper to taste (this recipe is especially good if you use cracked peppercorns.)

Place uncovered in a preheated 375 degree oven for approximately 30 minutes. Turn chicken over and baste with juices in pan. (If you need more liquid, add ½ cup water or white wine). Roast another 20-30 minutes until chicken is tender.

Nutrition (per serving): 395 calories

Saturated Fat	15g
Total Fat	66g (75% of calories)
Protein	48g (24% of calories)
Carbohydrates	2g (1% of calories)
Cholesterol	235mg
Sodium	184mg

My Notes and Recipe Variations

Chicken

Chicken or Turkey Kabob

Serves   4

Preparation   :20   Cook   :10   Stand   :00   Total   :30

Ingredients

1	pound boneless turkey breasts, cut in 1-inch cubes (or chicken breast)
1	zucchini, cut in ¼-inch slices
1	yellow squash, cut in ¼-inch slices
1	onion, cut in eighths
3	tablespoons vegetable oil
2	large green bell peppers, cleaned and seeds removed
12	whole mushrooms, cleaned
¼	cup Dijon mustard
¼	cup lemon juice
2	tablespoons olive oil
½	teaspoon salt
½	teaspoon pepper
1	tablespoon ready-to-use garlic, minced
½	teaspoon onion salt

Cut turkey or chicken into 1 inch cubes. In a large plastic freezer bag (or air tight container) add ¼ cup lemon juice, ¼ cup Dijon mustard, salt, pepper, garlic, onion salt and oil. Add chicken or turkey and place in refrigerator for 30 minutes.

Remove meat from refrigerator and put onto a skewer, alternate chicken or turkey, mushrooms, onions, zucchini, squash and bell peppers.

Pour remaining marinade in a cup to be used while cooking kabobs. Place kabob on barbecue rack 5-8 inches from coals or heat. Heat should be medium. Brush kabob with marinade. Grill about 5 minutes. Turn kabob and add more marinade; grill an additional 5 minutes longer; until chicken or turkey is cooked.

To keep kabob moist, you may wish to add a small pan of water over coals or heat source and below kabob. You can also cook the kabob in your broiler.

Nutrition (per serving): 371 calories

Saturated Fat	3g
Total Fat	20g (49% of calories)
Protein	30g (32% of calories)
Carbohydrates	17g (18% of calories)
Cholesterol	46mg
Sodium	2312mg

My Notes and Recipe Variations

Chicken

Cornish Hens with Wild Rice Stuffing

Serves   4

Preparation   :10   Cook   1:20   Stand   :00   Total   1:30

Ingredients

4	Rock Cornish game hens
½ to ¾	cups long grain rice, cooked
½ to ¾	cups wild rice, cooked
1	cup mushrooms, diced
1	small onion, diced
1	teaspoon rosemary (optional)

giblets, from Cornish hens

Cook rice according to package directions. While rice is cooking, clean the Cornish hens and remove the giblets. Place giblets and necks in a small saucepan and cover with water. Bring to a boil, then reduce heat to a simmer and cook until giblets are done.

Stuffing

When giblets are cooked, remove from heat, and chop. Add cooked white and wild rice, to a bowl. Add diced mushrooms, giblets and onions and mix well. Add 1 teaspoon rosemary and salt and pepper to taste. This is for the stuffing.

Sprinkle the body cavity of each hen with salt and pepper. Take stuffing mixture and fill each hen. Tie the legs together so stuffing does not fall out. Place hens, breast side up, in a roasting pan and brush with butter. Bake at 375 degrees for about 1 hour-1½ hours, until hens are cooked. (Check package directions, based upon the size of the hens.) If there is any remaining stuffing, place around the hens for the last ½ hour or so, while baking.

Nutrition (per serving): 725 calories

Saturated Fat	14g	
Total Fat	61g	(49% of calories)
Protein	54g	(19% of calories)
Carbohydrates	91g	(32% of calories)
Cholesterol	430mg	
Sodium	131mg	

My Notes and Recipe Variations

Chicken

Florentine-Chicken, Pork or Veal

Serves 4

Preparation :15 Cook 1:00 Stand :00 Total 1:15

This is a similar recipe to Bracioli, except spinach is used instead of parsley. You can also use boneless veal slab and make a roast.

Ingredients

4	chicken breasts, veal cutlets, pork tenderloin
4	slices provolone cheese, (for a tangier flavor used grated, hard provolone)
1	10 oz. package frozen spinach, thawed and well drained
4	fresh garlic cloves, crushed or minced

salt, and pepper to taste

Using meat tenderizer, pound meat until tender and about ⅛ inch thick. Lightly brush olive oil over meat.

Place a piece of provolone on each piece of meat. Take ¼ of spinach and place on cheese, spreading evenly. Sprinkle with garlic, add salt and pepper to taste. Roll lengthwise and tie roll with thread or string so it will not fall apart while baking.

Sprinkle with parsley and paprika. Bake in a 350 degree oven for 45 minutes to 1 hour. (If using boneless veal and you will make a rolled roast, take all ingredients and spread evenly. Roll meat from short end. Tie well with thread or string. Bake in a 350 degree oven for 30 minutes a pound. Ovens may vary.

Nutrition (per serving): 272 calories

Saturated Fat	1g
Total Fat	3g (11% of calories)
Protein	57g (84% of calories)
Carbohydrates	4g (6% of calories)
Cholesterol	137mg
Sodium	305mg

My Notes and Recipe Variations

Chicken

Fried Chicken

Serves   6

Preparation   :15   Cook   :30   Stand   :00   Total   :45

Ingredients

1	broiler-fryer chicken, cut up
1½	cups unbleached flour
1	teaspoon salt
1	teaspoon black pepper
1	teaspoon paprika
½	teaspoon garlic powder
1	egg
2	tablespoons water
½	cup bread crumbs

Add flour, salt, pepper, paprika and garlic powder to a freezer bag. Shake well.

Add ¼ of chicken and shake to well coated. Remove and place on waxed paper. Repeat with remaining chicken.

In a bowl beat 1 egg with water. Using a deep skillet (about 3 inches in height–preferably a cast iron skillet) add oil to about 1½ inches (about 2–3 cups). Heat oil over medium heat until very hot.

Take flour coated chicken and place in egg, then dip back into flour mixture to ensure well coated. Place in hot oil (making sure not to burn yourself). Cook 3-4 pieces at a time. Brown chicken on one side (about 4-5 minutes). Reduce heat to low, turn chicken over and finish cooking (another 4-5 minutes). Remove from oil and place on oven proof plate. (Do Not Stack)

Place in a warm oven (about 250 degrees) to finish cooking about 30-40 minutes. Repeat with remaining chicken pieces.

Variation:

If you like a more heavily breaded chicken, add flour, salt, pepper, paprika, garlic powder to a bowl and add enough water to make a very thick batter. Use a large saucepan, instead of the skillet and make sure that the oil is filled about 2-3 inches high. Place 2 to 3 pieces of chicken at a time in the hot oil, turning occasionally so as to not burn. Continue as above.

Nutrition (per serving): 529 calories

Saturated Fat	12g	
Total Fat	28g	(48% of calories)
Protein	38g	(29% of calories)
Carbohydrates	31g	(23% of calories)
Cholesterol	195mg	
Sodium	684mg	

My Notes and Recipe Variations

Chicken

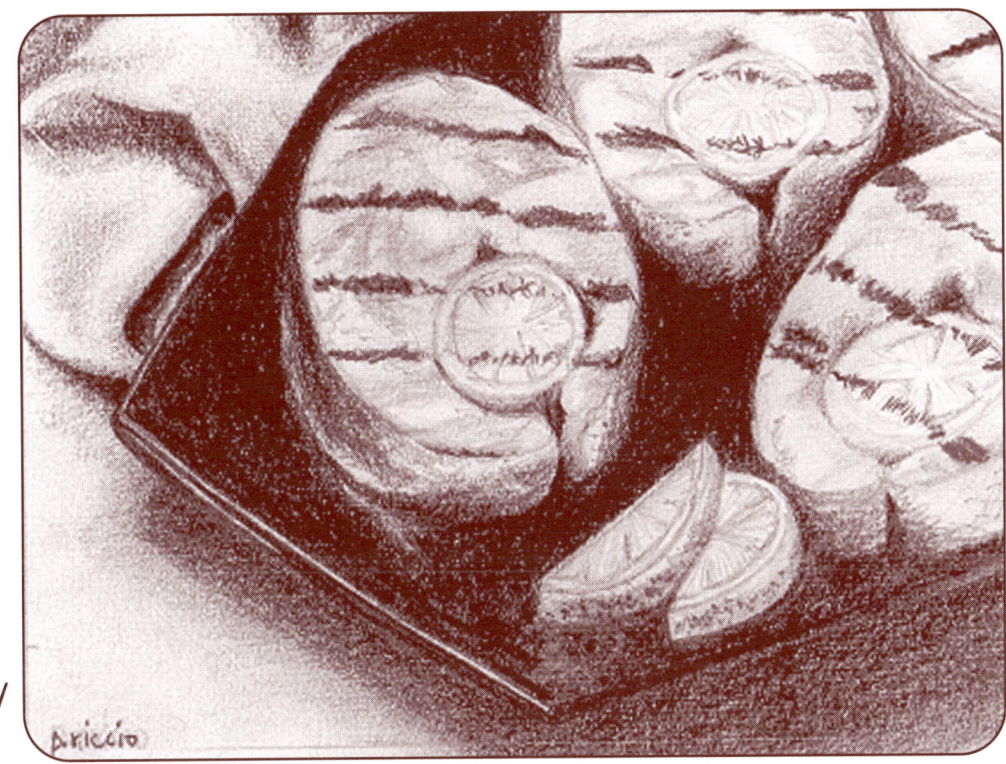

Fish and Seafood

a.riccio

Nutrition (per serving): 202 calories

Saturated Fat	1g
Total Fat	5g (21% of calories)
Protein	31g (62% of calories)
Carbohydrates	9g (17% of calories)
Cholesterol	73mg
Sodium	682mg

My Notes and Recipe Variations

Fish and Seafood

Nutrition (per serving): 318 calories

Saturated Fat	6g
Total Fat	32g (12% of calories)
Protein	213g (34% of calories)
Carbohydrates	347g (55% of calories)
Cholesterol	28mg
Sodium	371mg

My Notes and Recipe Variations

Fish and Seafood

Nutrition (per serving): 505 calories

Saturated Fat	3g
Total Fat	15g (26% of calories)
Protein	32g (25% of calories)
Carbohydrates	58g (46% of calories)
Cholesterol	90mg
Sodium	153mg

My Notes and Recipe variations

Fish and Seafood

Nutrition (per serving): 110 calories

Saturated Fat	0g
Total Fat	1g (11% of calories)
Protein	20g (73% of calories)
Carbohydrates	4g (16% of calories)
Cholesterol	35mg
Sodium	335mg

My Notes and Recipe Variations

Fish and Seafood

73

Nutrition (per serving): 403 calories

Saturated Fat	8g
Total Fat	15g (35% of calories)
Protein	48g (48% of calories)
Carbohydrates	18g (18% of calories)
Cholesterol	148mg
Sodium	454mg

My Notes and Recipe variations

Fish and Seafood

Nutrition (per serving): 195 calories

Saturated Fat	2g
Total Fat	15g (71% of calories)
Protein	3g (6% of calories)
Carbohydrates	12g (24% of calories)
Cholesterol	2mg
Sodium	2963mg

My Notes and Recipe Variations

Fish and Seafood

Nutrition (per serving): 498 calories

Saturated Fat	2g
Total Fat	17g (48% of calories)
Protein	25g (8% of calories)
Carbohydrates	25g (45% of calories)
Cholesterol	40mg
Sodium	767mg

My Notes and Recipe Variations

Fish and Seafood

Nutrition (per serving): 343 calories

Saturated Fat	1g	
Total Fat	5g	(14% of calories)
Protein	39g	(46% of calories)
Carbohydrates	34g	(40% of calories)
Cholesterol	313mg	
Sodium	452mg	

My Notes and Recipe Variations

Fish and Seafood

Shrimp Scampi

Serves   6

Preparation :15   Cook :20   Stand :00   Total :35

Ingredients

½	pound butter
¼	cup extra light olive oil
½ to 1	tablespoon garlic, minced (as desired)
2	teaspoons chives, chopped
¼	cup dry white wine
¼	cup finely diced celery
20 to 30	large shrimp

In a large saute pan, add oil and heat. Add garlic and saute for several minutes, until garlic permeates oil. Add butter and melt. Mix well. Add white wine and stir. Bring to a boil, then reduce heat to simmer. Add shrimp and chives. Cook until shrimp is tender and cooked. Serve with a side of pasta, salad and homemade bread. Use the homemade bread to dip into the scampi sauce.

Nutrition (per serving): 461 calories

Saturated Fat	21g
Total Fat	41g (81% of calories)
Protein	19g (17% of calories)
Carbohydrates	1g (1% of calories)
Cholesterol	225mg
Sodium	451mg

My Notes and Recipe Variations

Fish and Seafood

White Fish Baked with Lemons and Dill

Serves   4

Preparation   :10   Cook   :45   Stand   :00   Total   :55

Ingredients

1½	pounds fish fillets, (flounder, sole, cod, whiting)
1	lemon, thinly sliced
2	tablespoons fresh dill weed, chopped
1	teaspoon salt
1	teaspoon black pepper
2	fresh garlic cloves, chopped
1	tablespoon olive oil
2	tablespoons lemon juice (optional)
2	tablespoons water

Brush a 9x12 baking dish with olive oil. Place ½ sliced lemon over the bottom of the baking dish. Lay fish on top of lemon. Cover the fish with the remaining lemon and garlic. Sprinkle salt and pepper and sprinkle the dill over the top. Mix the lemon juice and water together and pour over top of fish. Bake in a 375 degree oven for approximately 45 minutes, until fish flakes easily.

Variation:

For a different flavor you may wish to try sage or rosemary in place of the dill.

Deep Fried Smelts

Serves   8

Preparation :10 Cook :20 Stand :00 Total :30

The holidays were never complete without adding fried smelts to our evening celebration for Christmas or New Year's eve.

Ingredients

2 to 3	pounds smelt, cleaned and gutted
1 to 2	eggs, slightly beaten
2	tablespoons water
1	cup flour
1	teaspoon salt
$\frac{1}{4}$	teaspoon pepper

oil, for deep frying

Place flour, salt and pepper in a bowl and mix well. Beat eggs with water in a separate bowl. Place smelt in egg mixture, then dip in flour and put into hot oil. Deep fry for 2 to 4 minutes on all sides. Remove with slotted spoon and place on paper towels to remove excess oil. Keep warm in a 175 degree oven while rest of fish is cooking. Serve warm.

Variation to Batter:

1	egg yolk, beaten
1	cup ice water
$\frac{3}{4}$	cup unbleached flour

Mix egg yolk and water until smooth. Add flour and stir or whisk well. (Batter will be runny). Chill several hours (or overnight). Heat oil. Dip smelts in batter (only a thin film will adhere). Deep fry for 2-4 minutes when fish rises to surface, remove. Serve immediately.

Seafood Pasta Primavera

Serves   6

Preparation   :10   Cook   :25   Stand   :00   Total   :30

Ingredients

2 to 3	tuna steaks, (or swordfish) cut into bite sized pieces
10 to 12	Italian tomatoes, peeled and cut into quarters. (about 3 pounds)
6	ounces pea pods
4	scallions, diced
1	small onion, diced
1	cup mushrooms, sliced
½	cup Romano cheese
2	7-inch long zucchinis, diced
2	7-inch long yellow squash, diced
1	pound fettuccine, cooked according to package directions
3	tablespoons extra light olive oil
3	fresh garlic cloves, chopped
2	tablespoons Italian flat-leaf parsley, chopped
½	cup dry white wine
½	cup water
1	teaspoon oregano

In a large skillet, add oil and heat. Add garlic, onions and tomatoes and saute until tender. Add remaining vegetables and parsley and saute until pea pods are tender crisp (about 2 minutes). Remove vegetables from skillet (leave broth in pot). Add ½ cup dry white wine and ½ cup water and bring to a boil. Add tuna or swordfish pieces and cook for 2 minutes. Reduce to a simmer. Cook an additional 3-4 minutes, until fish is done and flakes easily when tested with a fork. Return vegetables to the skillet and mix well. Remove from heat. Toss with pasta. Sprinkle with Romano cheese.

Sole Florentine

Serves 4

Preparation :15 Cook :35 Stand :00 Total :50

You can also use flounder for this delicious meal

Ingredients

4	sole fillets, (or flounder)
4	slices provolone cheese, (or 2 tablespoons finely grated)
1	10 oz. package frozen spinach, thawed and well drained
4	fresh garlic cloves, crushed or minced

salt and pepper, to taste
olive oil, to brush fish

Rinse fillets and pat dry with paper towel. Place a sheet of waxed paper on counter or table. Lightly brush with olive oil. Place fish fillets on waxed paper and lightly brush with olive oil. In a small bowl, add spinach, salt and pepper and garlic. Mix well. (If using grated Romano or provolone cheese, add to spinach mixture and mix well.) If using slices of provolone, place one slice on each piece of fish. If need be, cut to fit fillets. Spoon $\frac{1}{4}$ of spinach mixture onto each piece of fish and spread evenly.

Roll fish from short end and place rolled fish (seam side down) in a lightly oiled baking dish and sprinkle lightly with Paprika. Place in a 350 degree oven covered for approximately 15 minutes. Remove cover and continue baking or another 10-15 minutes, until tender and flaky; making sure that fish does not overcook.

Serve with fresh steamed vegetables. You may also serve with a light wine sauce or hollandaise sauce and sprinkle lightly with paprika.

Stuffed Flounder or Rolled Flounder

Serves   4

Preparation   :15   Cook   :30   Stand   :00   Total   :45

Ingredients

4	flounder fillets, (or fresh whole headless flounder, cleaned and scaled
4	tablespoons butter, melted
½	cup bread crumbs
2	8 oz. canned clams, drained
2	tablespoons fresh parsley
1	fresh garlic clove, minced (or 1 teaspoon minced already prepared garlic)
½	teaspoon pepper
⅓	cup dry sherry

Source: Merlo Bailey

Preheat oven to 350 degrees.

Mix all ingredients EXCEPT fish, together. Lightly grease a baking dish (about 15x9x3) or spray with non-stick vegetable oil.

Take each flounder and stuff with filling (or spread filling onto fillet, then lightly roll fillet, beginning at wide end. Place stuffed fish in the baking dish. (If using fillets, you may wish to use a square baking dish.)

Bake for 30-45 minutes, until fish is tender. (Rolled fillets will take longer than full fish.

Swordfish or Tuna Steaks

Serves   4

Preparation :05   Cook :20   Stand :00   Total :25

This simple to use recipe can be made on the top of the stove or on a grill.

Ingredients

3 to 4	tablespoons SEAFOOD SEASONING
$\frac{1}{4}$	cup milk
$\frac{1}{4}$	cup light olive oil, or vegetable oil

Seafood Seasoning
1 teaspoon of each:

dried oregano	salt
chili powder	garlic powder
parley	black pepper
cayenne pepper	onion powder
celery salt	ground basil
ground thyme	paprika (2 teaspoons)

Place swordfish in a shallow bowl and cover with milk. Let sit for 20 minutes, making sure swordfish is drenched. Place up to $\frac{1}{4}$ cup of seafood seasoning in a separate shallow bowl. Heat cast iron skillet and lightly coat skillet with olive oil. Heat until slightly smoking. Remove swordfish from milk and coat well with seafood seasoning on all sides. Place in skillet for 2 minutes. Turn swordfish over for another 2 minutes (using a metal spatula). Reduce heat to medium and continue cooking for 4-5 minutes on each side, until swordfish is no longer pink in center. Serve immediately.

This same recipe can also be used for grilling swordfish. Place foil on grill and prick with a fork to make many holes. Lightly coat foil with olive oil and heat thoroughly. Place seasoned swordfish on foil and cook until done. (I often use a special rack made for fish on the grill, so the full flavor of the grilling can come through without the foil).

Swordfish with Eggplant Sauce

Serves   4

Preparation   :10   Cook   :20   Stand   :00   Total   :30

Ingredients

Eggplant Sauce
1	small onion
1½	pounds eggplant
¼	cup extra virgin olive oil
1	16 oz. can tomato sauce
1	cup dry red wine
2	garlic cloves, minced
6	Italian tomatoes, peeled and cubed
4	Swordfish filets

salt and pepper, to taste

Eggplant Sauce:

Clean the bell pepper and cut into bite sized pieces. Cut the ends off the eggplant and peel. Cube the eggplant into bite sized pieces. Cut and dice onion. Place the tomatoes into a pot of boiling water and let sit for 2-3 minutes. Remove from water and peel off the skin. Cube the tomatoes.

Using a large skillet (12 inch at least), add olive oil and heat. Add garlic and saute. Add onion and saute until tender. Add tomato sauce, wine and cubed eggplant and tomatoes. Simmer for 20-25 minutes, until well blended and vegetables are tender.

Swordfish:

In a medium to large cast iron skillet, add 2 to 3 tablespoons of olive oil and 1 tablespoon of minced garlic. Heat and saute garlic. Add sliced swordfish and saute until tender and done (about 8-10 minutes). Add eggplant sauce and serve.

Breaded Shrimp

Serves   8

Preparation   :05   Cook   :20   Stand   :00   Total   :25

Aunt Mary Jane always made the best fried shrimp around and I couldn't wait to visit with them during the holidays

Ingredients

3	pounds large shrimp, cleaned and deveined
1 to 2	cups arrowroot, (or flour)
2 to 3	eggs, well beaten (or Egg beaters)
2	cups seasoned bread crumbs

oil, for frying

Source: Auntie Mary Jane

Clean and devein shrimp (use large or jumbo shrimp). In a bowl or large plate, place 1 cup of arrowroot. In a separate bowl add the eggs and beat well. Add bread crumbs in a separate bowl or large plate. Place several pieces of shrimp in the arrowroot and coat well. Dip coated shrimp in the eggs, then in the seasoned bread crumbs. (To make your own seasoned bread crumbs, add 2 cups of regular bread crumbs, $1/2$ teaspoon garlic powder, 1 tablespoon dried parsley and 2 to 4 tablespoons of Romano cheese and a pinch of salt. Mix well.)

Place several cups of oil (Cannola is best) in a large skillet (electric fry pan or frier) and heat to about 340 degrees. Place several pieces of shrimp in pan and brown until tender. Remove shrimp from skillet and place on a paper towel to absorb excess oil. Repeat until all shrimp is cooked. Do not overcook, especially if you will keep warm in an low oven.

To keep cooked shrimp warm, while remaining shrimp is cooking, turn oven to 225 degrees. Place several pieces of paper towel on an oven proof platter. Place shrimp on paper towel and put in oven.

Fried Calamari

Serves   4

Preparation   :15   Cook   :15   Stand   :00   Total   :30

There is nothing like fresh fried Calamari. You can often obtain cleaned and prepped fresh Calamari from your grocer's seafood section. Serve these with lemon or the white crab sauce and lemon dip.

Ingredients

10	ounces fresh or frozen squid, already cleaned
2/3	cup unbleached flour
1	teaspoon salt
1	egg
2	Tbs. water
2	tablespoons Cannola oil

You will need about 2 cups of Cannola oil for frying the Calamari. Cut squid into 1/2 inch sections. Beat egg and add water. Mix well. Place squid in egg then in flour. Then gently place in hot oil and fry for about one minute. Being careful not to overcook. Overcooking will cause squid to become rubbery.

Nutrition (per serving): 233 calories

Saturated Fat	2g	
Total Fat	11g	(41% of calories)
Protein	16g	(28% of calories)
Carbohydrates	18g	(32% of calories)
Cholesterol	271mg	
Sodium	650mg	

My Notes and Recipe variations

Cappelini with Calamari

Serves   6

Preparation   :00   Cook   :00   Stand   :00   Total   :00

Ingredients

¼	cup olive oil
3	cloves garlic, finely chopped
1	pound Italian tomatoes (pomodora), finely chopped
¼	cup dry white wine
¼	cup Italian flat-leaf parsley, chopped
1	pound pasta, Capellini, prepare as directed
1	pound calamari, cleaned and cut into rings
½	teaspoon crushed red pepper flakes
1	cup basic vegetable stock

Place water in pot for pasta. Sauce will take about at long as it takes to boil the water for the pasta.

Using a large cast iron skillet, heat the oil over a low to medium heat. Add the garlic and saute. Add the vegetable stock, tomatoes, wine salt and pepper and parsley. Bring the sauce to a boil. Simmer until sauce thickens.

While the sauce is simmering add the pasta to the boiling water and cook according to package directions. (Capellini usually takes about 2-4 minutes).

While pasta is cooking, add the calamari to the sauce and simmer for about 2 minutes. DO NOT OVERCOOK the calamari or it may become rubbery in consistency rather than easy to chew.

Remove sauce from heat, drain pasta, add sauce to pasta and serve immediately.

Shrimp Italiano

Serves   4

Preparation   :10   Cook   :30   Stand   :00   Total   :40

Aunt Jeannie was a wonder in the kitchen. Try this shrimp recipe for a change of pace over rice or pasta.

Ingredients

20	medium-size shrimp, cleaned and deveined
2	fresh garlic cloves, chopped
2	tablespoons light olive oil
1	28 oz. can canned stewed tomatoes, pureed in blender
½	cup white wine
2	dashes Tabasco sauce
1	teaspoon salt
½	teaspoon white pepper
½	teaspoon oregano, Optional
½	teaspoon dried basil, Optional

Source: Aunt Jeannie

In a large skillet, add olive oil and garlic. Saute until tender. Add fresh, cleaned shrimp and quickly cook until done (when shrimp turns white). Do not overcook. Remove shrimp from pan. Add stewed tomatoes, wine, Tabasco sauce, salt and pepper (oregano and/or basil, if desired). Bring to a boil, then reduce heat to medium and cook another 20 minutes. Add shrimp.

Serve over white steamed rice or fettuccine.

Stuffed Calamari in Tomato Sauce

Serves   6

Preparation   :15   Cook   1:00   Stand   :00   Total   1:15

Try for a variety and side dish to great pasta.

Ingredients

2	pounds Calamari
2	cups ricotta cheese
2	eggs
1	tablespoon dried parsley
¼	cup Romano cheese
1	teaspoon salt
1	teaspoon black pepper
3 to 4	cups SPAGHETTI SAUCE – MEATLESS (Try the recipe on pages 378, 398 or 392)

Prepare meatless spaghetti sauce as directed. In medium sized bowl, add ricotta cheese, eggs, Romano cheese, salt and pepper.

Mix well. Stuff each Calamari with the cheese mixture. Use toothpicks to close the ends to make sure no cheese runs out.

Place some sauce in the bottom of a glass baking dish. Place stuffed Calamari on bottom of pan. Cover with a little more sauce. Bake in a 350 degree oven for 45 to 60 minutes until Calamari is tender.

Nutrition (per serving): 262 calories

Saturated Fat	2g
Total Fat	11g (38% of calories)
Protein	16g (24% of calories)
Carbohydrates	23g (35% of calories)
Cholesterol	201mg
Sodium	347mg

My Notes and Recipe Variations

Fish and Seafood

Nutrition (per serving): 180 calories

Saturated Fat	1g
Total Fat	8g (38% of calories)
Protein	9g (20% of calories)
Carbohydrates	14g (31% of calories)
Cholesterol	53mg
Sodium	1145mg

My Notes and Recipe variations

_____
_____
_____
_____
_____
_____
_____
_____
_____
_____
_____
_____
_____
_____
_____
_____

Fish and Seafood

Nutrition (per serving): 324 calories

Saturated Fat	8 g
Total Fat	16g (44% of calories)
Protein	36g (45% of calories)
Carbohydrates	9g (11% of calories)
Cholesterol	468mg
Sodium	618mg

My Notes and Recipe variations

Fish and Seafood

Beef, Pork, and Other Meat Recipes

Homemade Sausage

Serves   4

Preparation   :10   Cook   1:00   Stand   72:00   Total   73:10

Ingredients

1	pound lean ground beef
1	pound pork, ground
2	teaspoons meat tenderizer
½	teaspoon mustard seed
½	teaspoon marjoram
½	teaspoon garlic powder
½	teaspoon sage
1	teaspoon cracked peppercorns
1	tablespoon fennel seeds
1	cup water
2	teaspoons salt
1	tablespoon crushed red pepper, Optional
2	teaspoons paprika, Optional

Source: Grandma Lil

Mix all ingredients together (you can use all beef or all pork). Mix well. Put into sausage casings (or lay out a piece of foil and place meat mixture in center. Shape into a long rope about 1½ inch thick. Roll up in foil and place in refrigerator for about 3 days, so meat absorbs all of the flavors. Use sausage for pizza, or leaving wrapped in foil, boil in water for 1 hour and cool. Cut into bite sized pieces and place in tomato (or spaghetti) sauce the last 15 minutes of cooking, so it can absorb some of the tomato flavor.

Nutrition (per serving): 464 calories

Saturated Fat	12g
Total Fat	31g (61% of calories)
Protein	43g (38% of calories)
Carbohydrates	2g (1% of calories)
Cholesterol	159mg
Sodium	1328mg

My Notes and Recipe variations

Beef, Pork, and Other Meat Recipes

Barbecue Pork or Beef

Serves   4

Preparation   :10   Cook   :10   Stand   8:00   Total   8:20

Ingredients

1½	pounds pork, beef, lamb cut into cubes
1	cup unbleached flour
1	teaspoon salt
1	teaspoon coarsely ground black pepper
1	teaspoon Anaheim chili peppers
1	teaspoon Szechuan pepper oil
2	scallions, finely diced
2	tablespoons sesame seeds
¼	cup olive oil
3 to 4	cloves finely chopped garlic

Mix all ingredients together EXCEPT meat and sesame seeds. Place marinade in a small airtight container and add meat. Marinade overnight. Place several pieces of meat on a wooden skewer (3 or 4 pieces per skewer). Place sesame seeds on a plate. Roll skewered meat in sesame seeds. Place skewers on a hot grill and cook for 5-7 minutes, until done. You can also broil these, but must turn frequently to prevent burning.

Nutrition (per serving): 394 calories

Saturated Fat	5g
Total Fat	15g (35% of calories)
Protein	39g (40% of calories)
Carbohydrates	25g (25% of calories)
Cholesterol	111mg
Sodium	699mg

My Notes and Recipe Variations

Beef, Pork, and Other Meat Recipes

Bracioli-Chicken, Pork or Flank Steak

Serves   4

Preparation :15 Cook 1:00 Stand :00 Total 1:15

Ingredients

4	slices provolone cheese, sandwich style, medium to sharp
4	boneless chicken breasts, veal cutlets, pork tenderloin, flank steak
1	teaspoon oregano, approximate, to sprinkle on
4	fresh garlic cloves, chopped
4	teaspoons Italian flat-leaf parsley, chopped, plus extra to sprinkle over meat
1	tablespoon Romano cheese, grated

salt, and pepper to taste
olive oil, to brush on meat

Using a meat tenderizer, pound the chicken breast, pork or veal to tenderize and flatten to about ⅛ inch thick. (If you are using flank steak, cut into 4x6 inch pieces and tenderize).

Using pastry brush, brush one side of meat with olive oil. Place piece of provolone cheese over meat (or sprinkle sharp provolone). Sprinkle some oregano, ¼ of garlic and 1 teaspoon parsley over cheese, making sure it is spread evenly. Grate or shake a little Romano cheese over mixture.

From narrow end begin rolling meat up. Using thread tie the meat once lengthwise and twice across narrow ends to make sure no ingredients fall out. In a large skillet, add a little olive oil. Saute meat on all sides until lightly browned.

Variation 1:
When browned, add spaghetti sauce or Marinara sauce to cover (you can even use stewed Italian tomatoes with spices). Simmer in sauce for 1 hour, or until done.

Variation 2:
After browning the meat, place in a baking dish. Sprinkle a little parsley, salt and pepper to taste and a little paprika (over chicken or pork, only) and bake in a 350 degree oven for 45

minutes to 1 hour. Serve with a green salad and vegetables.

Nutrition (per serving): 259 calories

Saturated Fat	1g
Total Fat	4g (13% of calories)
Protein	55g (85% of calories)
Carbohydrates	1g (2% of calories)
Cholesterol	138mg
Sodium	269mg

My Notes and Recipe Variations

Beef, Pork, and Other Meat Recipes

Braised Short Ribs or Spare Ribs

Serves   6

Preparation   :15   Cook   3:30   Stand   :00   Total   3:45

Ingredients

3	pounds short ribs
2	medium sweet onion
1	teaspoon salt
1	teaspoon pepper
2	cups water
6	carrots, sliced
4	large potatoes
1	cup dry red wine

In a large skillet, brown the ribs on all sides. Remove from skillet and place in a large roasting pan or oven proof Dutch oven. Add water, wine, onion, salt and pepper. Stir well and make sure ribs are coated. Bake covered in a 350 degree oven for 2½ hours. Stirring occasionally and turning ribs over. Cook until ribs are almost done (fork-tender). Add carrots and potatoes for remaining 30 to 45 minutes.

This recipe can also be made on the stove, using a large Dutch oven. After browning the ribs, add water, wine, onion, salt and pepper. Reduce heat to low and simmer for 3 hours (adding more water as necessary to keep the ribs moist and free from burning). Add vegetables and cook for an addition 30-45 minutes. Serve with a green salad.

Nutrition (per serving): 682 calories

Saturated Fat	10g	
Total Fat	24g	(31% of calories)
Protein	50g	(29% of calories)
Carbohydrates	67g	(39% of calories)
Cholesterol	134mg	
Sodium	586mg	

My Notes and Recipe Variations

Beef, Pork, and Other Meat Recipes

Flank Steak Roll-ups

Serves   4

Preparation   :15   Cook   :20   Stand   :00   Total   :35

Ingredients

1½ to 2	pounds flank steaks
1½	cups mozzarella cheese, (or provolone) grated
1	cup Italian flat-leaf parsley, chopped (or spinach)
1	teaspoon salt
1	teaspoon black pepper
¼	cup Romano cheese
4	cloves garlic, chopped

Using a meat tenderizer, pound the flank steak into ⅛ inch thick. Cut the flank steak into 1 to ½ inch thick slice lengthwise to obtain a 10-12 inch strip. (if need be use two 5 or 6 inch strips end-to-end).

In a separate bowl, mix remaining ingredients well. Place all ingredients on top of meat. Begin rolling steak from one end to the other. Tie with string or thread to secure.

Bake in a 350 degree oven for approximately 20 minutes, until meat is done. Do not let meat touch sides of pan or each other. Remove and serve with salad and vegetable.

Preparation time will increase or decrease, depending on whether or not you have your friendly neighborhood butcher help you out with the meat preparation.

Nutrition (per serving): 447 calories

Saturated Fat	14g
Total Fat	29g (58% of calories)
Protein	44g (39% of calories)
Carbohydrates	4g (3% of calories)
Cholesterol	127mg
Sodium	933mg

My Notes and Recipe Variations

Beef, Pork, and Other Meat Recipes

Italian Meatballs

Serves   16

Preparation   :20   Cook   :45   Stand   :00   Total   1:05

Ingredients

2	pounds lean ground beef
2	large eggs
1½	cups bread crumbs
¼	cup Romano cheese, grated
1	teaspoon salt
1	teaspoon black pepper
1	tablespoon dried parsley
1	teaspoon garlic powder

In large bowl add ground beef. Make a hole (or well) in center and add the eggs, salt, pepper and parsley. Mix well. Add bread crumbs and grated cheese (you may substitute Parmesan cheese for a different flavor). Mix well. Take enough meat (about the size of a golf ball) and moving it between both hands form into a ball shape. Carefully place meatballs as you roll into the spaghetti sauce. Repeat with meat mixture until all meat is used. Cook 45 minutes to 1 hour in the sauce. Remove from sauce.

Suggestion:

You may remove the cooked meatballs and drain. When they are dry, place in a freezer bag and put into freezer ~ making sure that the meatballs lie flat. You may then have meatballs whenever you desire. These meatballs make a great hot sandwich on Italian or French bread.

NO BREAD CRUMBS??? Try this: Take 6-8 slices of bread. Toast well. Placed toasted bread in a food processor and grind. Or place toasted bread in a plastic bag and using fist break the bread. Measure for correct amount.

Nutrition (per serving): 199 calories

Saturated Fat	10g	
Total Fat	26g	(60% of calories)
Protein	25g	(25% of calories)
Carbohydrates	15g	(15% of calories)
Cholesterol	142mg	
Sodium	557mg	

My Notes and Recipe Variations

Liver and Onions

Serves   2

Preparation   :10   Cook   :25   Stand   :00   Total   :35

Great served with garlic mashed potatoes, gravy and green beans.

Ingredients

2	slices calves liver, about ¾ inch thick each
2 to 3	large yellow onions, julienne
½	pound thick bacon, cut into 1 inch pieces
¼	cup unbleached flour
½	cup milk

salt and pepper, to taste

In large skillet (preferably cast iron), add bacon and cook until well done. Remove bacon and reserve grease. Add onions to hot skillet and saute until tender brown. Remove onions.

Place some bacon grease in skillet and heat. In a bowl, add flour, salt and pepper. In a separate bowl, place milk. Place liver in milk and coat well. Place liver in flour and coat well on all sides. Place liver in skillet with bacon grease and cook for 2 minutes. Turn carefully and cook another 2 minutes. Reduce to medium low heat. Brown liver slowly on both sides. (The thicker slices will take a little longer). (Cook for 4-5 minutes on one side, turn over). Continue cooking until done. (Check by cutting into center). Liver should not be pink. Be careful to NOT overcook or liver will dry out. Place onions on top and cook an additional 5 minutes to reheat onions. Remove and serve immediately.

Smashed red potatoes with a little garlic and a tossed green salad compliment this meal.

Nutrition (per serving): 843 calories

Saturated Fat	25g	
Total Fat	68g	(73% of calories)
Protein	17g	(8% of calories)
Carbohydrates	41g	(19% of calories)
Cholesterol	86mg	
Sodium	1061mg	

My Notes and Recipe Variations

Beef, Pork, and Other Meat Recipes

Manzo al Italiana (Italian Beef)

Serves   8

Preparation   :10   Cook   3:00   Stand   :00   Total   3:10

Ingredients

4	pounds Beef Rump Roast, rolled
1	bunch Italian flat-leaf parsley
4	fresh garlic cloves, crushed
2	tablespoons flour
4	cups water
4	beef bouillon cubes
1	teaspoon ready-to-use garlic, chopped
1	teaspoon oregano, Optional

salt and pepper, to taste

Source: Grandma Lil

Make six slits in the top of the roast (fatty side) and insert bunch of parsley into two of the slits. Place 1 garlic glove into each of the remaining four slits. Salt and pepper. Place roast, fat side up in a roasting pan. Roast on 350 degrees for about 2- 2 1/2 hours or until beef medium (Beef will continue to cook when placed in gravy). Remove roast from pan and place on a cutting board and allow to cool. (Make sure cutting board has grooves to catch any juices). Once cooled, slice the beef with an electric or manual slicer (or with a very sharp knife). into very thin slices. Place in pan of hot gravy and let simmer over a low flame until heated through.

While roast is cooling, make the gravy. Place roasting pan on the top of stove and remove most of the grease from the drippings remaining in pan. Place the pan over a low heat and sprinkle 2 heaping tablespoons of flour into the pan. Blend with the back of a spoon (or with wire whisk) until a thick paste is formed. Slowly add about 4 cups of water, stirring and blending constantly. Add four beef bouillon cubes, (if need for more flavor) salt and pepper to taste and chopped garlic. Let simmer over heat, stirring occasionally. (Add more water if needed). Add sliced beef, as directed above. Allow beef to heat through.

Serve with a green vegetable, or place in a crusty roll to make a beef sandwich. Serve with sauteed green peppers or Pepperoni Fritti.

Nutrition (per serving): 306 calories

Saturated Fat	3g	
Total Fat	8g	(22% of calories)
Protein	53g	(69% of calories)
Carbohydrates	6g	(8% of calories)
Cholesterol	129mg	
Sodium	599mg	

My Notes and Recipe variations

Beef, Pork, and Other Meat Recipes

Meatballs

Serves 15

Preparation :20 Cook :45 Stand :00 Total 1:05

Ingredients

1	pound lean ground beef
1	egg
½	teaspoon salt
½	teaspoon pepper
1	small onion, Optional
1	teaspoon dried parsley
¼	cup Romano cheese
1	teaspoon garlic powder
¼	cup cold water, (or dry red wine)
1	cup bread crumbs

Mix all ingredients together well. Make balls about the size of golf balls. Place meatballs in tomato sauce for 45 minutes. If meat is not lean, you may wish to place in oven on a cookie sheet and bake for 20 minutes in a 350 degree oven to remove excess grease. You can also make the meatballs, and remove from sauce and freeze for future use.

Nutrition (per serving): 114 calories

Saturated Fat	3g	
Total Fat	7g	(57% of calories)
Protein	7g	(25% of calories)
Carbohydrates	5g	(18% of calories)
Cholesterol	39mg	
Sodium	169mg	

My Notes and Recipe variations

Pepper Steak with Rice

Serves 6

Preparation :10   Cook :45   Stand :00   Total :55

Ingredients

2	pounds round steaks, cut into strips about 2 inches long and ¼ inch thick
1	cup water
4	large green bell peppers
1	small sweet onion, diced
1	cup dry red wine
2	tablespoons extra virgin olive oil, or cannola oil
2	cups cooked rice

Using a meat mallet, pound meat to tenderize. Cut into julienne strips. In a large skillet (preferably cast iron), add oil and heat. Lower to a medium to low heat add steak pieces. Brown lightly on both sides. Add wine, water, tomato sauce. Mix well. Saute (or simmer) until meat is tender (20-30 minutes). Add stewed tomatoes and break with a spoon; add onions. Simmer for 10 minutes. Add bell peppers and continue to simmer for 10-15 minutes, until tender.

Serve over white rice.

Nutrition (per serving): 432 calories

Saturated Fat	11g	
Total Fat	33g	(46% of calories)
Protein	50g	(31% of calories)
Carbohydrates	37g	(23% of calories)
Cholesterol	143mg	
Sodium	125mg	

My Notes and Recipe Variations

_____
_____
_____
_____

Salisbury Steak with Onion Mushroom Gravy

Serves 8

Preparation :10   Cook :45   Stand :00   Total :55

Ingredients

2	pounds lean ground beef
2	eggs
1	large sweet onion, finely diced
1 to 2	fresh garlic cloves, minced
¼	cup Romano cheese, grated, Optional
½ to 1	cup bread crumbs, Optional
1	cup sliced mushrooms

Place all ingredients, except mushrooms, in a bowl and mix well. Shape meat into a loaf and slightly round the top. Place a baking rack inside of a baking dish and cover with foil. Prick holes in foil and place meat on top so excess fat will drain. Place in a preheated 375 degree oven for 20 minutes. While meat in cooking, make the gravy. In a medium saucepan, add 1 can of beef broth and 1 can of water. Dice a small onion and slice mushrooms. Add to the broth mixture and bring to a light boil. Reduce heat to a simmer. In a small covered container, add 1 cup of water and 2 to 3 tablespoons of flour. Shake well, making sure there are no lumps. Slowly pour the flour mixture, stirring constantly, into the heated beef broth. Continue stirring while cooking and gravy thickens.

Remove meat from oven. Carefully slice the meat into ¾ inch slices. Lay each slice in a baking dish. Cover Salisbury steak with some gravy. Return to oven and continue cooking until done (about 10-15 minutes.)

Serve with mashed potatoes and a vegetable.

Nutrition (per serving): 325 calories

Saturated Fat	79g	
Total Fat	198g	(69% of calories)
Protein	177g	(27% of calories)
Carbohydrates	28g	(4% of calories)
Cholesterol	1105mg	
Sodium	761mg	

My Notes and Recipe Variations

Beef, Pork, and Other Meat Recipes

Sauerbraten

Serves 10

Preparation :15 Cook 3:30 Stand 96:00 Total 99:45

This Marinated Beef is great served with potato pancakes, dumplings or noodles.

Ingredients

4	pounds boneless chuck roast, (blade or arm)
2	cups vinegar
2	cups water
1	large onion, sliced
1/4	cup sugar
2	teaspoons salt
10	peppercorns
3	whole cloves
1	bay leaf
1	lemon, rinsed and cut into 1/4 inch slices
2 to 3	tablespoons butter
1/4	cup butter

Source: Aunt Julie and Ms. Bertelle

Place meat in a large, clean 4 quart bowl and set aside. In a 2 quart saucepan, add 2 cups vinegar, 2 cups water, sliced onion, 1/4 cup sugar, 2 teaspoons salt, peppercorns, cloves and bay leaf. Mix well and heat without boiling. Pour the hot mixture over meat and allow to cool. Add lemon slices. Cover and set in refrigerator. Marinate for 4 days, turning meat at least once each day.

After marinading, remove meat from bowl, and drain. Strain and reserve marinade.

Heat Dutch oven over low heat with 2 to 3 tablespoons butter, until marinated. Add roast and slowly brown on all sides over medium heat. Slowly add 2 cups of reserved marinade (reserve remaining marinade for gravy). Bring liquid to a boil. Reduce heat; cover Dutch oven or kettle tightly and simmer 2½ to 3 hours, or until meat is tender when pierced with a fork. Add more of the marinade if necessary. The liquid surrounding meat should be simmering, NOT boiling, at all times. When cooked, remove meat to a warm platter and keep warm. Pour cooking liquid from kettle and set aside for gravy.

Gravy:

Melt 1/4 cup butter in Dutch oven. Blend in 1/4 cup flour

using a fork or wire whisk. Heat, stirring constantly, until butter and flour mixture bubbles and is golden brown. Stirring constantly, add 3 cups reserved marinade (add enough hot water to reserved liquid and marinade to make 3 cups).

Return to heat. Bring to boil; cook rapidly stirring constantly until gravy thickens. Cook 1 to 2 minutes longer. Remove from heat. Stirring constantly with fork or wire whisk, add in $\frac{1}{2}$ cup thick sour cream. Return to heat and cook mixture over low heat for approximately 3 to 5 minutes, until thoroughly heated —DO NOT BOIL— Stir constantly. Serve meat and gravy with potato pancakes, noodles or dumplings.

Nutrition (per serving): 627 calories

Saturated Fat	23 g	
Total Fat	51 g	(74% of calories)
Protein	31 g	(20% of calories)
Carbohydrates	11 g	(7% of calories)
Cholesterol	151 mg	
Sodium	660 mg	

My Notes and Recipe Variations

Beef, Pork, and Other Meat Recipes

Sausage and Peppers

Serves 4

Preparation :10 Cook :45 Stand :00 Total :55

This recipe is just as good cooked on the grill or in your oven in a roasting pan.

Ingredients

4	crusty French bread hoagie rolls
4	fresh Italian sausage, links
3	green bell peppers
1	large onion

In roasting pan, add sausage and $\frac{1}{2}$ cup water. Cover roasting pan and bake in a 375 degree oven for $\frac{1}{2}$ hour. Reduce heat to 350, remove cover and continue to cook for 20 minutes (until meat is cooked and lightly browned). During cooking process, stir meat so all sides will be browned. The last 10 minutes of cooking, add green peppers and onion (cut in strips). Stir and cook.

Place the bread (cut lengthwise) in the oven for 10 minutes to get crunchy. Serve sausage on roll with green peppers and onions.

If you like, make Marinara sauce and place over sausage.

Nutrition (per serving): 396 calories

Saturated Fat	0g
Total Fat	1g (7% of calories)
Protein	3g (12% of calories)
Carbohydrates	17g (81% of calories)
Cholesterol	1mg
Sodium	78mg

My Notes and Recipe Variations

Beef, Pork, and Other Meat Recipes

Steak with Mushroom and Wine Sauce

Serves   4

Preparation   1:00   Cook   :30   Stand   :00   Total   1:30

Ingredients

4	tenderloin or fillet steaks
½	pound mushrooms, sliced
½	cup dry red wine
½	cup celery, diced
¼	cup extra virgin olive oil
2 to 4	tablespoons butter
3	cloves fresh garlic, finely minced

salt and pepper, to taste

Place steaks in a freezer bag (or airtight container with lid), cover with wine and add garlic. Place in refrigerator and let sit for 45-60 minutes. Clean mushrooms and slice, clean celery and dice (about 4-6 stalks). In a large skillet (12 inch skillet) add 2 tablespoons olive oil and heat. Reserve wine marinade. Brown steaks on both sides, using a fork or tongs to turn them. Cook until done (3-4 minutes on each side for rare). Remove steaks from skillet. Using the same skillet, add 1-2 tablespoons butter in pan and add mushrooms and celery. Saute until tender. Place the wine that was used for marinade in the skillet. Stir and scrap pan to dislodge any brown bits from pan. Pour mixture over steaks and serve hot.

Nutrition (per serving): 196 calories

Saturated Fat	5g
Total Fat	20g (89% of calories)
Protein	1g (3% of calories)
Carbohydrates	4g (8% of calories)
Cholesterol	16mg
Sodium	173mg

My Notes and Recipe variations

Beef, Pork, and Other Meat Recipes

Tenderloin Tips in Wine Sauce

Serves   6

Preparation :20   Cook :50   Stand :10   Total 1:20

Easy 2 pot recipe for a delicious, low fat meal.

Ingredients

1½ to 2	pounds Beef Tenderloin, cut into bite sized pieces (or stew beef)
1	cup celery, dice in small bite sized pieces
2	each large green bell peppers, cut into bite sized pieces
1	cup mushrooms, cut into small slices
1	each medium sweet onion, chop into bite sized pieces, Optional
2 to 3	cups dry red wine
1	teaspoon sea salt
1	teaspoon white or black pepper
1	10 oz. can tomato sauce
1	10 oz. can water
3	cloves fresh garlic cloves, finely chopped

Place 1 or 2 tablespoons olive oil or spray large skillet with non-stick spray, when heated add tenderloin tips/stew beef and garlic, saute until the meat is browned. Add 1½ cups wine and ½ cup water. Cover and cook over medium to low heat until liquid is almost evaporated (at least ½ of liquid should be absorbed/evaporated). Add 1 cup wine, tomato sauce and 1 cup water, cook until ½ liquid is evaporated. (While meat is continuing to cook, prepare rice for 6 servings, as package directs).

Add all vegetables, salt and pepper to taste and cook an additional 5-10 minutes, until vegetables are soft, but still a little crunchy.

Serve over rice, with a salad

Nutrition (per serving): 337 calories

Saturated Fat	8g
Total Fat	20g (53% of calories)
Protein	31g (37% of calories)
Carbohydrates	9g (11% of calories)
Cholesterol	96mg
Sodium	769mg

My Notes and Recipe Variations

Center Cut Pork Chops with Onions and Home Fries

Serves   4

Preparation   :10   Cook   :45   Stand   :00   Total   :55

An easy to make quick meal. Served with pan fried potatoes, makes a delicious meal.

Ingredients

4	center cut pork chop
4	large sweet onion, sliced or julienne
2	tablespoons olive oil
2	garlic cloves, finely diced

parsley
salt and pepper, to taste

Using a large cast iron skillet, melt lard (or Crisco) and saute garlic until tender. Clean potatoes and slice. Place in skillet and cook until tender. Stirring to ensure the potatoes do not stick to pan. Potatoes will develop a slight crust and get slightly browned. Remove from heat and keep warm.

Add 2 tablespoons (or butter) to skillet and add onions and saute until tender. Remove onions from pan. Place pork chops in skillet and cook (about 10 minutes on each side) over a medium heat. Reduce heat to low and add onions to top of pork chops.

Sprinkle with salt, pepper and parsley and stir. Let simmer for an additional 10 minutes, until pork is tender.

Serve with potatoes, corn or greens and a salad

Nutrition (per serving): 335 calories

Saturated Fat	3g
Total Fat	14g (38% of calories)
Protein	25g (30% of calories)
Carbohydrates	27g (32% of calories)
Cholesterol	62mg
Sodium	172mg

My Notes and Recipe variations

Beef, Pork, and Other Meat Recipes

Pork Chops with Sauerkraut

Serves   6

Preparation   :15   Cook   1:10   Stand   :00   Total   1:25

Ingredients

6	each pork chops
1	package sauerkraut, (approximately 4 cups or 32 oz)
1	cup water
¼-½	cup unbleached flour
1	teaspoon black pepper
2	medium sweet onion, diced
½	teaspoon caraway seeds, Optional

Source: Aunt Jeannie

Place ¼-½ cup of flour in plastic bag. Add pork chops and shake until they are well coated. In a large skillet, add 2 tablespoon lard or (Cannola oil); coat pan well. Add pork chops and lightly brown. Remove pork chops from skillet and place in a rectangular oven proof pan. In a bowl, mix remaining ingredients and sauerkraut. Mix well. Place sauerkraut and juice over pork chops.

Optional Gravy:

Add ¼ cup flour to a 10 oz (or larger) jar. Add 1 cup water and shake well, ensuring that there are no lumps. Using the skillet the pork chops were cooked in, reheat skillet and slowly add the water and flour mixture to the pork juices, until a gravy forms. Pour the gravy through a strainer onto the pork chop and sauerkraut mixture.

Bake in a 350 degree oven for at least 1 hour (until pork chops are tender).

Suggestion:

Serve with a green salad.

Nutrition (per serving): 407 calories

Saturated Fat	10g	
Total Fat	27g	(60% of calories)
Protein	25g	(24% of calories)
Carbohydrates	16g	(15% of calories)
Cholesterol	87mg	
Sodium	73mg	

My Notes and Recipe Variations

Beef, Pork, and Other Meat Recipes

Pork Tenderloin - Breaded

Serves   4

Preparation   :15   Cook   :20   Stand   :00   Total   :35

Serve hot with vegetables and a salad. These fried pork tenderloins can also be used in Parmigiana or used cold in a sandwich with Italian or Rye Bread, served with Italian peppers and onions in tomato sauce.

Ingredients

1	pound pork tenderloin, cut ¼ inch thick
1	cup unbleached flour
1	cup bread crumbs
1	egg, beaten with 2 Tbs water
¼	cup water
¼	cup oil

salt and pepper, to taste

Using a meat tenderizer, pound pork tenderloin pieces into ⅛ inch thick pieces. Put flour and bread crumbs in a separate bowl. This will be used to dip the pork. Beat egg with water in a separate bowl. Dip pork into water, flour, then egg, then bread crumbs. Place on waxed paper. Continue this process until all pork is coated.

Place in refrigerator for 1 hour to set.. Add oil to large skillet (preferably cast iron). Heat over medium heat. Add pork to hot skillet (enough to cover bottom of skillet). Cook for 2 minutes on one side, turn over and brown other side (3-5 minutes) until pork is tender. Remove from oil and place on paper towels to drain excess oil.

Nutrition (per serving): 524 calories

Saturated Fat	4g	
Total Fat	25g	(43% of calories)
Protein	33g	(25% of calories)
Carbohydrates	42g	(32% of calories)
Cholesterol	117mg	
Sodium	348mg	

My Notes and Recipe variations

Beef, Pork, and Other Meat Recipes

Roast Pork

Serves 8

Preparation :10   Cook   1:45   Stand   :00   Total   1:55

Ingredients

3 to 5	pounds boneless pork loin roasts
8 to 10	fresh garlic cloves, peeled and sliced in half lengthwise
1	tablespoon sea salt (coarse)
2	tablespoons coarsely ground black pepper

Fat side up, using a very sharp paring knife, cut 12 slits in roast on top (just large enough to place garlic and should be different depths). Push 1 or 2 pieces of sliced garlic clove into each hole. Lightly brush the top with vegetable oil. Place salt and pepper in a plate and roll the top of the roast into the mixture.

Place roast, fat side up in a baking dish or roasting pan. Cook in a 350 degree oven for approximately $1\frac{1}{2}$ to $1\frac{3}{4}$ hours (about 30-35 minutes per pound). If using a meat thermometer it should register 172-175 degrees. Remove pork from oven and let sit 15 minutes before slicing. (Pork will continue to cook during the resting time).

Variation:
Instead of place fresh garlic into the roast, place 1/4 C of granulated garlic in a plate. Dampen the roast with water. Roll the pork roast in the granulated garlic to coat well. Spray a little vegetable spray on the top and salt and pepper.

Place the roast in roasting pan and cook as directed, above.

NOTE: When garlic is used to coat a roast or chicken, the outer layer of the roast (or chicken) will appear 'pink', even though the inside is cooked.

Nutrition (per serving): 310 calories

Saturated Fat	7g
Total Fat	19g (55% of calories)
Protein	33g (43% of calories)
Carbohydrates	2g (3% of calories)
Cholesterol	109mg
Sodium	990mg

My Notes and Recipe Variations

Beef, Pork, and Other Meat Recipes

Stuffed Pork Chops - Apple

Serves   4

Preparation   :10   Cook   1:10   Stand   :00   Total   1:20

Ingredients

4	pork chops, with bone, 1 inch thick
2	large apples, peeled, cored and diced
1	teaspoon paprika
1	cup bread crumbs, or unflavored stuffing croutons
¼	cup dry sherry
1	egg

Cut pork chops in half, lengthwise to the bone, but not all the way through. In mixing bowl add all ingredients and mix well.

Stuff pork chop. Preheat oven to 350 degrees. Place pork chops on baking sheet (or in large baking dish on rack, making sure to not touch each other) and bake for 1 hour or until pork is cooked. Do not overcook or pork will become dry.

Serve with a German style potato salad, vegetables or tossed green salad.

Suggestion:
You may use 1 to 1½ cups of a chunky style applesauce in place of the fresh apple.

Nutrition (per serving): 535 calories

Saturated Fat	10g	
Total Fat	30g	(50% of calories)
Protein	28g	(21% of calories)
Carbohydrates	39g	(29% of calories)
Cholesterol	141mg	
Sodium	271mg	

My Notes and Recipe Variations

Beef, Pork, and Other Meat Recipes

Stuffed Pork Chops - Sausage

Serves   4

Preparation   :10   Cook   1:10   Stand   :00   Total   1:20

Over the years I have continuously modified this recipe with different spices for slightly different flavored meals. Get imaginative.

Ingredients

4	pork chops, with bone, cut 1 inch thick
2	Italian sausage, large links removed from casing
¼	cup Romano cheese
1	cup bread crumbs
1	fresh garlic clove, finely diced
¼	cup celery stalks, finely chopped
1	tablespoon Italian flat-leaf parsley, finely chopped

salt, and pepper to taste

In a mixing bowl, place sausage (removed from casing), add all ingredients and mix well. Using a very sharp knife, cut pork chop lengthwise to the bone (do not cut all the way through). Stuff enough sausage mixture inside so that the outer section shows approximately ½ to ¾ inch.

Place pork chops on a baking sheet or in a large baking dish with rack. Preheat oven to 350 degrees. Cook at least 1 hour and check to see that meat is done. Cook longer, if necessary, but ensure the pork does not dry out. Place under broiler, if desired for 5 minutes.

Serve with a potato and vegetable side dish. or a side of sauerkraut

Suggestion:
You may also use 1 pound of butcher made pork sausage.

Nutrition (per serving): 608 calories

Saturated Fat	16g
Total Fat	44g (65% of calories)
Protein	34g (22% of calories)
Carbohydrates	19g (13% of calories)
Cholesterol	128mg
Sodium	750mg

My Notes and Recipe Variations

Beef, Pork, and Other Meat Recipes

Stuffed Pork Loin Roast

Serves   10

Preparation   :10   Cook   2:00   Stand   :00   Total   2:10

Ingredients

3 to 5	pounds boneless pork loin roasts, (untie roast and lie flat on waxed paper)
2 to 3	fresh garlic cloves, diced
2	tablespoons parsley
1	egg
1	cup bread crumbs
1	cup pork sausages
1	teaspoon thyme, rosemary or sage

Untie roast and lie flat on waxed paper. Mix remaining ingredients in a bowl. Spread mixture evenly over flattened roast, in center. Re-roll the roast and tie with string to hold securely.

Bake in a 350 degree oven for about 1½ hours, until done or meat thermometer registers 175 degrees.

Nutrition (per serving): 336 calories

Saturated Fat	7g	
Total Fat	20g	(55% of calories)
Protein	30g	(36% of calories)
Carbohydrates	8g	(9% of calories)
Cholesterol	117mg	
Sodium	304mg	

My Notes and Recipe variations

Beef, Pork, and Other Meat Recipes

Veal in Sherry Sauce

Serves   4

Preparation   :20   Cook   :25   Stand   :00   Total   :45

This same recipe can be used by substituting chicken in place of the veal.

Ingredients

4	veal cutlets, pounded to $1/8$ inch thick
$1/2$	pound mushrooms, sliced
$2/3$	cup dry sherry, (if you prefer a sweeter taste, use sweeter sherry)
$1/4$	cup fresh parsley, chopped
1	teaspoon dried parsley
2	fresh garlic cloves, crushed
6	tablespoons butter
6	Swiss cheese, slices (optional)

Place sherry, mushrooms, parsley and garlic in an airtight container, shake well. Add veal and marinade for at least 30 minutes. Drain the liquid of the marinade into a measuring cup or small bowl. In a large skillet, melt the butter. Add veal and mushrooms (without liquid). Saute on all sides until done (about 3 minutes on each side). Add the marinade juice to the meat and bring to a boil. Reduce the heat and place the cheese slices on top of the meat. Cover and cook until cheese melts.

Nutrition (per serving): 312 calories

Saturated Fat	13g	
Total Fat	23g	(65% of calories)
Protein	22g	(28% of calories)
Carbohydrates	5g	(7% of calories)
Cholesterol	123mg	
Sodium	279mg	

My Notes and Recipe Variations

Beef, Pork, and Other Meat Recipes

Veal Parmigiana

Serves 6

Preparation :15 Cook 1:30 Stand :00 Total 1:45

For a more economical meal, you can use pork tenderloin and follow the same recipe. Often times, I have made the Parmigiana with pork and no one new the difference.

Ingredients

4	veal, sliced thinly (¼ inch thick)

SAUCES, DIPS & GRAVY - SPAGHETTI SAUCE - MEATLESS, about 2 cups

1	cup mozzarella cheese, grated
¼	cup Romano cheese
1	cup unbleached flour
1	egg, well beaten
1	teaspoon water
2	tablespoons olive oil
1	teaspoon salt
1	teaspoon black pepper
½	cup Romano cheese, grated

Partially freeze veal cutlets so they will be easier to slice. Cut each veal cutlet into ⅛ inch thick. Using a meat tenderizer, pound the veal to tenderize and further flatten. In a large bowl, add flour, salt, pepper. In a separate bowl, beat egg with 1 tablespoon of water. Heat a skillet and place 2 tablespoons olive oil in skillet. Dip the veal into the egg mixture, then the flour mixture; coating well. Place in heated skillet and cook over medium heat until lightly browned on all sides. Remove veal from skillet and place on paper towel to remove excess oil.

Use a baking dish of 9x12x3. Place a small amount of spaghetti sauce in bottom of dish. Carefully line the bottom with breaded veal. Alternate layers of sauce, veal, and cheese until all the meat is used. Add remaining sauce on top of veal and sprinkle mozzarella cheese on top. Bake in a 350 degree oven for 30-45 minutes, until veal is tender. Bon Appetito!

Speedier Preparation: Ask your butcher to prepare the meat for you

Nutrition (per serving): 230 calories

Saturated Fat	5g	
Total Fat	13g	(50% of calories)
Protein	10g	(18% of calories)
Carbohydrates	18g	(32% of calories)
Cholesterol	61mg	
Sodium	622mg	

My Notes and Recipe Variations

Beef, Pork, and Other Meat Recipes

Veal Piccata

Serves   4

Preparation   :15   Cook   1:30   Stand   :00   Total   1:45

This same recipe can be used with chicken.

Ingredients

1½	pounds veal cutlets, pounded to ⅛ inch thick
½	cup unbleached flour
1	egg, well beaten
½	teaspoon white pepper
1	teaspoon salt
½	cup dry white wine
3	tablespoons lemon juice
2	teaspoons capers, Optional
½	cup butter, or oil

Using a meat tenderizer, pound veal until ⅛ inch thick. Add flour, salt and pepper in a dish and mix well. Beat egg in a bowl. In a large skillet (preferably cast iron or non-stick) add ½ cup cannola oil. Heat. Place veal in egg, then in flour mixture and coat well. Place in hot skillet and cook on both sides until golden. Remove from skillet and place on plate.

Continue this until all veal is cooked. Lower heat and add wine, lemon juice and mix well, scraping sides and bottom to release browned flour. Bring to a boil. Reduce heat and simmer, stirring constantly until slightly thickened. If sauce does not thicken, add ¼ to ½ teaspoon more flour and mix well with a whisk.

Add capers and spoon over veal. Serve with lemon wedges.

Nutrition (per serving): 484 calories

Saturated Fat	16g	
Total Fat	29g	(54% of calories)
Protein	38g	(31% of calories)
Carbohydrates	14g	(11% of calories)
Cholesterol	250mg	
Sodium	976mg	

My Notes and Recipe variations

Veal Roast

Serves   8

Preparation :05   Cook 2:00   Stand :00   Total 2:05

Ingredients

3½ to 4   pounds boneless veal leg rump roast, (or veal shoulder roast)
½   teaspoon fresh thyme leaves
¼   teaspoon small fresh sage leaves
2   cups chicken broth
1   onion, finely chopped
2   fresh garlic cloves, smashed or sliced, Optional
salt, to taste

Source: Merlo Bailey

Place roast in a shallow roasting pan. Rub onto meat the thyme leaves, sage and garlic (optional). Sprinkle lightly with salt Place chopped onion around meat. Add ¼ cup of chicken broth Bake uncovered in a 325 degree oven for approximately 1 hour. Add an additional 1-1¼ cups chicken broth (use canned chicken broth, full strength) into bottom of pan. Stir, breaking loose any browned particles. Baste meat 1 or 2 times. Continue to cook at least another 1 hour (or until meat thermometer registers 170 degrees). Remove from oven when done. Remove meat to a serving platter and keep warm.

Set the roasting pan on the stove top and turn heat to high. Stir juices to dislodge brown particles and juice comes to a boil. Meanwhile, in a small container, add 1 tablespoon of cornstarch (or arrowroot) with 2 tablespoons water. Mix well. Using a whisk, stir the juices in the pan and add the flour mixture, a little at a time into the juices until the sauce is the consistency you desire. Pour gravy into a bowl. Spoon over sliced roast.

NOTE:

You may substitute a 2½ pound boned, rolled Pork Loin Roast, baking for 2 hours or until meat thermometer registers 180 degrees.

Nutrition (per serving): 216 calories

Saturated Fat	1g	
Total Fat	4g	(16% of calories)
Protein	43g	(79% of calories)
Carbohydrates	3g	(5% of calories)
Cholesterol	155mg	
Sodium	541mg	

My Notes and Recipe variations

Beef, Pork, and Other Meat Recipes

Veal Scaloppine

Serves 4

Preparation :20 Cook :30 Stand :00 Total :50

Ingredients

2	pounds veal, sliced thin
$1/3$	cup unbleached flour
2	teaspoons salt
$1/2$	teaspoon pepper
$1/3$	cup butter
2	fresh garlic cloves, minced
$1/2$	cup medium sweet onion, minced (or finely diced)
1	cup mushrooms, sliced
1	16 oz. can tomatoes, chopped

Flatten veal by using a meat tenderizer and pounding until very thin. In a bowl add flour and 1 teaspoon salt and pepper. Mix well Place veal in the flour and coat well. Using a large skillet, melt the butter on low heat. Add the veal and saute until lightly browned. Remove veal from skillet. Add garlic and onion to the butter in the pan. Cook until onion is tender. Add mushrooms, tomatoes and cook an additional 5-7 minutes. Add veal and continue to cook over low heat until veal is tender.

Serve over cooked spaghetti.

Nutrition (per serving): 464 calories

Saturated Fat	12g	
Total Fat	22g	(44% of calories)
Protein	49g	(42% of calories)
Carbohydrates	17g	(14% of calories)
Cholesterol	230mg	
Sodium	1538mg	

My Notes and Recipe Variations

Serves   8

Preparation   :15   Cook   :45   Stand   :15   Total   1:15

Ingredients

4	slices of bread
2	eggs, separated
½	pound morrel mushrooms (shitake may be substituted)
⅔	cup milk
1½	cup sour cream
1	lg onion, finely minced
2	lb ground beef
1	tbs fresh dill finely chopped
½	tsp tarragon
salt and pepper to taste	

Cut crusts from bread and place in a small bowl. Cover the bread with milk. Let stand. In the meantime, in a large skillet, saute the minced onions. Remove from heat.

In a large bowl, combine the ground beef, lightly beaten egg yolks, bread mixture, onion, dill, tarragon, salt and pepper. Let stand

Beat 2 egg whites until they form soft peaks. Fold the beaten egg whites into the beef mixture. Make small, bite sized meatballs and place on a plate. When you finish forming the meatballs, roll lightly in flour.

In a large skillet, using the ½ cup of butter, over a medium heat, brown the meatballs. When meatballs are done browning, remove from heat.

While the meatballs are browning, heat 3 tablespoons of butter in another skillet and saute ½ pound of sliced mushrooms until lightly browned. When mushrooms are browned, spoon over meatballs and stir. Once they are mixed, add the sour cream, making sure to coat the meatballs well and simmer in the mixture. Place a cover partially over the pan and simmer over a low heat for about 30 minuts, sitrring occassionaly.

Serve with fresh steamed string beans and a hearty bread and salad.

Nutrition (per serving): 478 calories

Saturated Fat	14g
Total Fat	35g
Protein	26g
Carbohydrates	14g
Cholesterol	159 mg
Sodium	245 mg

My Notes and Recipe variations

Pasta

Baked Ziti

Serves 8

Preparation :10 Cook 1:15 Stand :00 Total 1:25

Ingredients

1	pound ziti macaroni, cooked according to package directions
2	cups skim milk ricotta cheese
$\frac{1}{4}$	cup Romano cheese, grated
2	cups low fat low sodium mozzarella cheese, shredded
4	cups spaghetti sauce
1	egg
1	tablespoon dried parsley
1	teaspoon salt
1	teaspoon black pepper

Cook ziti until firm (slightly undercook). In a large mixing bowl, while pasta is cooking, add ricotta cheese, Romano cheese, salt, pepper, parsley and egg. Mix well until all ingredients are fully blended.

When pasta is cooked, drain completely and return to pot you cooked in. Add the ricotta cheese mixture to ziti and stir well. Next add $1\frac{1}{2}$ cups of mozzarella and 3 cups of spaghetti sauce. Mix well.

In a large baking pan (2 inches in height) add ziti mixture. Pour additional sauce on top. Bake in a 375 degree oven for 45 minutes, uncovered. This will allow the ziti to finish cooking and absorb additional sauce. Sprinkle remaining mozzarella cheese on top and return to oven for another 20 minutes, or until cheese turns golden.

Nutrition (per serving): 456 calories

Saturated Fat	4g
Total Fat	11g (21% of calories)
Protein	29g (25% of calories)
Carbohydrates	61g (53% of calories)
Cholesterol	51mg
Sodium	1195mg

My Notes and Recipe variations

Pasta

Capellini Pomodoro (Angel Hair Pasta with Tomatoes and Garlic)

Serves   4

Preparation :15   Cook :10   Stand :00   Total :25

Pasta is an all time favorite and one low in calories, if you watch what you put 'on top'.

Ingredients

2½	cups chicken broth
6 to 10	Italian tomatoes (POMODORO), diced
2	tablespoons olive oil
2	tablespoons Romano cheese, grated
1	pound pasta, capellini, cook per package directions
¼	teaspoon oregano, ¼ to ½ teaspoon depending on taste
3	cloves garlic cloves, peel and finely chop
1	bunch Broccoli, clean and use Florets (or us frozen broccoli pieces), Optional
3	each carrots, sliced, Optional
20	each pea pods, Optional

Prepare Pasta as directed. Once pasta is put into the boiling water, in a large skillet add olive oil, diced tomatoes and chopped garlic (add oregano if using). Saute for approximately 2 minutes, until tomatoes are coated with oil and garlic and they are warm. (If using other vegetables, add at this time and saute until light and crisp).

Drain Pasta and put oil, tomato mixture over the pasta and toss lightly. Sprinkle with Romano cheese. This recipe will serve 4 without the added vegetables, 6 if the vegetables are added. Salt and pepper to taste.

Serving Suggestion:
Serve hot with a large salad and home-made bread.

Nutrition (per serving): 233 calories

Saturated Fat	2g
Total Fat	9g (35% of calories)
Protein	8g (13% of calories)
Carbohydrates	30g (52% of calories)
Cholesterol	40mg
Sodium	949mg

My Notes and Recipe Variations

Pasta

Cavatelle *(Cheese Pasta)*

Serves   6

Preparation   :30   Cook   :20   Stand   :00   Total   :50

Ingredients

2½	cups unbleached flour
2	eggs
1	egg yolk
1	cup ricotta cheese
1	teaspoon salt

In a large bowl, add ricotta, eggs, egg yolk and salt. Beat well. Gradually begin adding flour (about ⅓ to ½ cup at a time). Mix well. Add more flour, mix. Continue this process until you make a soft dough. Turn dough onto a lightly floured surface and knead until very smooth and not sticky. (10-15 minutes). Separate dough into 6-8 pieces. Using your hands, roll each piece into a 15-18 inch rope shape. Cut each rope into ½ inch pieces. Press in center of the dough to flatten, while continuing to press on dough, roll away from you to form a curled piece of dough. Lay on lightly floured baking sheet and let dry for 1½ hours. Or (The dough should be rolled about ½ inch in diameter and long). Cut the dough into ½ to ¾ inch lengths. Using a fork, place the fork, tine side up on the table. Place one piece of the dough on the center of the fork. Using your thumb, place your thumb in the middle of the dough, press firmly in the center and roll the dough off the tines and flip. This will curl the dough and make an impression. Place the rolled dough onto a lightly floured cookie sheet. When all of the dough is used, you can either cook the Cavatelle (after drying for 20 minutes) or place it in the freezer. When frozen, place in a freezer bag for future use.

To cook, fill a large pot with water. Over a high heat, heat water with 1 teaspoon salt and 1 tablespoon olive oil. and bring to a rapid boil. Add cavatelli and cook until tender (8-10 minutes). Cavatelli will rise to top. Drain well and serve with favorite sauce.

Variation:

Cavatelli are great made in a salad with broccoli or zucchini, olive oil and spices. Cook cavatelli as directed until done. Drain and rinse with cold running water until cooled. Drain, add vegetables as desired.

Nutrition (per serving): 290 calories

Saturated Fat	4g
Total Fat	8g (26% of calories)
Protein	13g (17% of calories)
Carbohydrates	41g (57% of calories)
Cholesterol	126mg
Sodium	449mg

My Notes and Recipe Variations

Pasta

Gniocchi (Polish-Mashed Potato Pasta)

Serves   6

Preparation   :30   Cook   :20   Stand   :00   Total   :50

Gniocchi is a very filling meal. To be served with Spaghetti Sauce. This is the Polish variation of the Italian Cavatelli.

Ingredients

3	large Idaho potatoes, cooked and mashed
2	eggs
1½	cups unbleached flour
1	teaspoon salt

In a large mixing bowl mash (or use a mixer) the cooked potatoes. Add 2 eggs and mix well. Slowly begin adding the flour (¼ cup at a time). Mix well. Continue adding the flour until the dough does not stick to your hands any longer. Depending on the type of flour used, you may use more or less.

When dough is made, cut pasta into 6 or 8 pieces. With floured hands, roll each piece into a 12-15 inch rope (The dough should be rolled about ½ inch in diameter and long). Cut the dough into ½ to ¾ inch lengths. Using a fork, place the fork, tine side up on the table. Place one piece of the dough on the center of the fork. Using your thumb, place your thumb in the middle of the dough, press firmly in the center and roll the dough off the tines and flip. This will curl the dough and make an impression. Place the rolled dough onto a lightly floured cookie sheet. When all of the dough is used, you can either cook the Gniocchi (after drying for 20 minutes) or place it in the freezer. When frozen, place in a freezer bag for future use.

Cooking time:

Boil a pot of water with 1 teaspoon of salt and 1 tablespoon of oil. When the water is brought to a full boil, add the

Gniocchi and stir. When the Gniocchi rises to the top of the water, they are done (about 10 minutes). Serve with spaghetti sauce (meat or meatless).

Nutrition (per serving): 307 calories

Saturated Fat	1g
Total Fat	2g (6% of calories)
Protein	9g (12% of calories)
Carbohydrates	63g (82% of calories)
Cholesterol	71mg
Sodium	426mg

My Notes and Recipe Variations

Pasta

Lasagna

Serves 15

Preparation :15 Cook 3:00 Stand :30 Total 3:15

Holidays in our family wouldn't be the same without lasagna. My grandfather loved cheese lasagna while we enjoyed a meat and cheese lasagna. Mom use to split the lasagna pan and make half with cheese only and half with meat and cheese.

Ingredients

SPAGHETTI SAUCE- with or without MEAT

2	pounds lasagna noodles
6	pounds ricotta cheese, (use more or less, as desired)
1/4	cup Pecorino Romano cheese
3	eggs
3	tablespoons Italian flat-leaf parsley, finely chopped (or 2 tablespoons dried)
1	teaspoon salt
1	teaspoon black pepper
2	pounds lean ground beef, (omit if making cheese or veggie lasagna)

Make meatless spaghetti sauce as directed. In large pot, add ground beef and saute until cooked. Remove about 1/3 to 1/2 of spaghetti sauce and add to ground beef. Cook as directed.

In a large bowl, add ricotta, Romano, eggs, parsley, salt and pepper. Mix well. 20 minutes before sauce is cooked, fill a large pot with water and add 1 teaspoon salt and 2 tablespoons olive oil. Bring water to a boil. Add lasagna noodles. Slightly undercook.

In a large lasagna pan (or baking dish), place several ladles of meatless spaghetti sauce and coat well. Add one layer of lasagna noodles. Next add a small layer of Ricotta cheese mixture over noodles, by adding spoonfuls and then lightly spreading it over noodles. Sprinkle with Mozzarella cheese. Spoon sauce over cheese mixture, (either meat, plain or 1/2 of each sauce). Add another layer of noodles and repeat the process. Depending on how large a pan you are using, you should be able to add at least 2 layers, preferably three. The very top of the lasagna should be covered with meatless sauce.

Bake in a 375 degree oven for 2 to 3 hours (longer, depending on how large a pan of lasagna is made and how thick the sauce was), until noodles are done and sauce is absorbed and cheese is 'set'. Remove from oven and let stand for at least 20 minutes so cheese sets.

Variation:

For a Veggie lasagna. You can use several small zucchini and yellow squash. Clean and slice to ¼ inch slices. Use squash and zucchini with each layer. You can use a cheese sauce instead of tomato sauce.

Nutrition (per serving): 719 calories

Saturated Fat	21g	
Total Fat	39g	(49% of calories)
Protein	41g	(23% of calories)
Carbohydrates	50g	(28% of calories)
Cholesterol	181mg	
Sodium	395mg	

My Notes and Recipe variations

Pasta

Linguine with Garlic and Oil

Serves   6

Preparation :15   Cook :25   Stand :05   Total :45

Ingredients

½	cup extra light olive oil
1	tablespoon fresh garlic cloves, chopped
12	ounces dry linguine or spaghetti, cook as package directs
½	cup fresh parsley, finely chopped, Optional
½	teaspoon salt
½	teaspoon black pepper

Cook linguine as directed on package. While pasta is cooking, heat oil in a skillet and add the chopped garlic. Saute until tender. Drain pasta. While pasta is draining, add oil and garlic to the pot. Pour pasta into pot and toss until well coated. You may add a little more oil, if needed. Sprinkle parsley (if desired), toss and serve.

Suggestions:

1. You can add small shrimp to the oil and garlic when sauteing (about 30) and cook until shrimp is done.

2. You can add various vegetables, such as pea pods, broccoli florets, cauliflower, julienned carrots for a different change of pace. Simply saute the vegetables in the olive oil and garlic until tender and toss with pasta.

3. A flavorful alternative is finely cut prosciutto ham, sliced and diced, pea pods, julienned carrots. Lightly saute the prosciutto, pea pods and carrots, then toss with linguine.

Nutrition (per serving): 374 calories

Saturated Fat	3g
Total Fat	19g (46% of calories)
Protein	7g (8% of calories)
Carbohydrates	43g (46% of calories)
Cholesterol	0mg
Sodium	200mg

My Notes and Recipe Variations

Pasta

Linguine con Prosciutto e Legumi
(Linguine with Prosciutto and vegetables)

Serves   6

Preparation :15   Cook :30   Stand :00   Total :45

Ingredients

1	pound linguine
1	pound spinach linguine
6	ounces Prosciutto, THINLY sliced and diced
2	fresh garlic cloves, slivered or chopped
2	teaspoons Italian flat-leaf parsley, chopped, Optional
½	pound snow pea pods, cleaned
½	cup broccoli florets, fresh
¼	cup Pecorino Romano cheese
¼	cup extra virgin olive oil
1	teaspoon salt
½	teaspoon black pepper
1	teaspoon crushed red pepper, Optional

Prepare linguine as package directs and cook until al dente. While pasta is cooking, in a large skillet, heat the Prosciutto (do NOT brown). Remove from heat. To the skillet add 2 tablespoons olive oil, garlic, parsley. Saute until tender. Reduce heat to low to medium and add vegetables; salt and pepper to taste. Cook for 2-3 minutes only, stirring constantly. Add Prosciutto. Remove from heat and cover. Vegetables will continue to cook.

When linguine is al dente, drain well and put in large serving bowl. Add ¼ olive oil and toss gently until well coated. Add vegetable mixture and ¼ cup Romano cheese. Toss and serve hot.

Variation:

Also see Linguine with Prosciutto and Peas for a different "sauce" and flavor.

Nutrition (per serving): 707 calories

Saturated Fat	3g
Total Fat	14g (18% of calories)
Protein	28g (16% of calories)
Carbohydrates	117g (66% of calories)
Cholesterol	12mg
Sodium	791mg

My Notes and Recipe Variations

Pasta

Manicotti Filling

Serves   6

Preparation   :15   Cook   1:30   Stand   :00   Total   1:45

Please see Ravioli Filling for ingredients. You will need to double the recipes, in some cases, depending on how many manicotti you wish to make.

Ingredients

SPAGHETTI SAUCE~MEATLESS

1	pound lean ground beef
1 to 2	10 oz. packages frozen chopped spinach, thawed and well drained
2 to 3	fresh garlic cloves, finely diced
$\frac{1}{4}$ to $\frac{1}{2}$	cup Romano cheese
$\frac{1}{2}$	cup mozzarella cheese, shredded, Optional
1 to 2	eggs

salt and pepper, to taste

Place a large pot of water with $\frac{1}{4}$ cup olive oil and bring to a boil. Place 10-12 manicotti/cannelloni shells in boiling water and cook for 8 to 10 minutes (DO NOT OVERCOOK shells should be slightly firm, not fully cooked). While shells are cooking, place ground beef and garlic in skillet and cook until done, using a wooden spoon to break meat into small pieces. Remove from skillet and drain well. Place meat and remaining ingredients in a bowl and mix well.

Drain shells and rinse under cool water to stop the cooking process. Line a rectangular baking dish with meatless spaghetti sauce. Using a small spoon or pastry bag stuff the shells with meat/spinach mixture. Lay each shell into baking dish. Cover tops of shells with sauce and sprinkle with mozzarella cheese.

Bake in a preheated 350 to 375 degree oven for about 1 to $1\frac{1}{2}$ hours, until sauce is absorb and shells are fully cooked.

Nutrition (per serving): 245 calories

Saturated Fat	7g
Total Fat	18g (66% of calories)
Protein	17g (28% of calories)
Carbohydrates	4g (6% of calories)
Cholesterol	96mg
Sodium	232mg

My Notes and Recipe variations

Pasta

Linguine with Prosciutto and Peas

Serves   8

Preparation   :10   Cook   :30   Stand   :00   Total   :40

If you don't care for peas, you can substitute broccoli, cauliflower or other vegetables.

Ingredients

1	pound linguine cooked according to package directions
1	small onion, diced
2	fresh garlic cloves, diced
½	stick butter, (or 2 tablespoons olive oil)
1	cup frozen peas
¼	cup Romano cheese
8	ounces Prosciutto, thinly sliced and diced
1	cup heavy cream cream

Using a large stock pot, fill with enough water to cook pasta. Bring to a rapid boil. Once the past begins to boil, add 1 teaspoon salt. Cook pasta for the time indicated on the package MINUS 2 minutes. At the last 2 minutes, add the frozen peas. When pasta is done, drain pasta and peas and place in a serving bowl large enough to toss with sauce.

While pasta is cooking, saute garlic in olive oil or butter, until tender, using a skillet. When garlic is tender, add Prosciutto and cook for 2 minutes. Add remaining ingredients and simmer for an additional 2-4 minutes (until cream and cheese mixture begins to thicken slightly). Drain pasta and peas when done. Place is large service bowl and pour/spoon sauce over pasta. Toss and service immediately.

Nutrition (per serving): 295 calories

Saturated Fat	2g
Total Fat	5g (15% of calories)
Protein	16g (22% of calories)
Carbohydrates	47g (64% of calories)
Cholesterol	17mg
Sodium	398mg

My Notes and Recipe Variations

Pasta

Ravioli-Dough

Serves   6 - 8

Preparation   :30   Cook   :10   Stand   1:30   Total   2:10

Basic pasta dough is generally made with 1 egg for each cup of flour used. You can alter the recipe, depending on how many hungry mouths you have to feed.

Ingredients

4	cups unbleached flour, sifted
4	eggs
½	teaspoon salt

Ravioli Filling (see pages 168-173)

In a large bowl, add sifted flour. In a separate bowl, beat the eggs until well blended. Make a well in the center of the flour and add the salt and eggs. Mix well, until all flour is absorbed. Turn out dough onto a lightly floured surface and roll into 2 pieces about $1/8$ inch thickness. (You can either use a ravioli form, press, glass or round cookie cutter to form ravioli). My grandmother used a glass about $2\frac{1}{2}$ to 3 inch in diameter. Lightly press the glass onto the dough to form the shape (do not cut through dough). Place filling in center of the ravioli (about 1 tablespoon). Cover the 'filled' dough with the second piece. Center the glass (or cutter) over the filled dough and cut. This will crimp and cut the ravioli. You may wish to use a fork to more tightly crimp the ravioli around the edges.

Let stand for $1\frac{1}{2}$ hours to dry slightly. Either freeze the ravioli or cook by placing in a pot of simmering salted water (about 5 minutes). Stir occasionally. Usually the ravioli will rise to the top when cooked. Serve with your favorite sauce.

Nutrition (per serving): 344 calories

Saturated Fat	1g
Total Fat	4g (11% of calories)
Protein	13g (15% of calories)
Carbohydrates	64g (74% of calories)
Cholesterol	142mg
Sodium	239mg

My Notes and Recipe Variations

Pasta

Ravioli Filling-Cheese

Serves   8

Preparation :10 Cook :00 Stand :00 Total :10

Ingredients

RAVIOLI-DOUGH Prepare dough as directed
3	cups ricotta cheese
¼	cup Romano cheese
½	teaspoon salt
½	teaspoon black pepper
2	eggs
1	tablespoon dried parsley

Prepare dough as directed. In a separate mixing bowl blend all the above ingredients until well mixed. Spoon into ravioli dough, crimp the ravioli as stated in the ravioli dough recipe.

Nutrition (per serving): 232 calories

Saturated Fat	9g
Total Fat	14g (56% of calories)
Protein	14g (25% of calories)
Carbohydrates	110g (19% of calories)
Cholesterol	120mg
Sodium	301mg

My Notes and Recipe variations

Ravioli Filling-Meat

Serves   8

Preparation   :30   Cook   :10   Stand   :00   Total   :40

Ingredients

RAVIOLI-DOUGH Prepare dough as directed

1	pound extra lean ground beef
¼	cup Romano cheese, grated
1	egg
1	tablespoon dried parsley, (or 2 teaspoons fresh chopped)
2	fresh garlic cloves, minced

In skillet saute meat and garlic until cooked. Drain in a strainer to remove excess moisture and fat. In large bowl, add beef, egg, garlic and cheese and mix well. Spoon into Ravioli dough as directed.

Nutrition (per serving): 193 calories

Saturated Fat	5g	
Total Fat	12g	(54% of calories)
Protein	14g	(29% of calories)
Carbohydrates	8g	(18% of calories)
Cholesterol	86mg	
Sodium	106mg	

My Notes and Recipe Variations

Ravioli Filling-Meat and Cheese

Serves   8

Preparation :30 Cook :15 Stand :00 Total :45

Excellent filling for cannelloni, stuffed shells or manicotti

Ingredients

RAVIOLI-DOUGH Prepare dough as directed
1	pound extra lean ground beef
2	cups ricotta cheese
¼	cup Romano cheese
1	cup mozzarella cheese, shredded
½	teaspoon salt
½	teaspoon black pepper
2	teaspoons dried parsley

In a skillet, brown ground beef until cooked. Drain using a strainer and remove excess fat and liquid. In a large bowl add all ingredients and mix well. Spoon into Ravioli dough, shells, cannelloni, manicotti shells. Cook as each recipe directs.

Nutrition (per serving): 303 calories

Saturated Fat	11g	
Total Fat	22g	(60% of calories)
Protein	23g	(28% of calories)
Carbohydrates	10g	(13% of calories)
Cholesterol	102mg	
Sodium	349mg	

My Notes and Recipe variations

Ravioli Filling=Meat and Spinach

Serves 8

Preparation :30 Cook :15 Stand :00 Total :45

Ingredients

RAVIOLI-DOUGH Prepare dough as directed
1   pound extra lean ground beef
2   10 oz. packages frozen chopped spinach
1   cup ricotta cheese
1   cup mozzarella cheese, grated or shredded
½   cup Romano cheese
½   teaspoon salt
½   teaspoon black pepper

In a skillet saute meat until cooked. Drain well removing excess fat and water. Defrost spinach and place in strainer.

Press down firmly on spinach to remove excess water. In a large bowl add all ingredients and blend well. Spoon into Ravioli dough/form. Cook as directed. Extra filling can be frozen in an air tight container for several months.

Nutrition (per serving): 296 calories

Saturated Fat	9g	
Total Fat	18g	(55% of calories)
Protein	21g	(29% of calories)
Carbohydrates	12g	(16% of calories)
Cholesterol	86mg	
Sodium	375mg	

My Notes and Recipe Variations

Pasta

Ravioli Filling=Spinach and Cheese

Serves   6

Preparation :10   Cook :00   Stand 1:00   Total   1:10

Ingredients

RAVIOLI-DOUGH Prepare dough as directed
2	10 oz. packages spinach, chopped, thawed, well drained
2	cups ricotta cheese
2	eggs
½	teaspoon salt
½	teaspoon pepper
¼	cup Romano cheese, grated

Thaw frozen chopped spinach. Place a paper towel (or coffee filter) in strainer and place thawed spinach. Press on spinach to remove excess moisture. In a large bowl, add spinach, cheeses, egg and salt and pepper. Mix well. Spoon onto ravioli dough as directed in dough recipe.

Nutrition (per serving): 199 calories

Saturated Fat	6g	
Total Fat	12g	(48% of calories)
Protein	13g	(26% of calories)
Carbohydrates	13g	(27% of calories)
Cholesterol	105mg	
Sodium	330mg	

My Notes and Recipe Variations

Ravioli Filling-Spinach and Pignoli

Serves 8

Preparation :10 Cook :00 Stand 1:00 Total 1:10

For a Great taste, try serving this ravioli with the Gorgonzola Sauce

Ingredients

RAVIOLI-DOUGH Prepare dough as directed

1¼	pounds frozen spinach, thawed and drained of all liquid
½	cup Pignoli, finely chopped (you may substitute chopped walnuts)
2	eggs, beaten

salt, Optional

Make dough according to directions. In a separate mixing bowl, add spinach, nuts and eggs. Mix well. Spoon into dough and make ravioli. Seal and crimp well.

Place on a cookie sheet lightly dusted with flour. If not using the ravioli immediately, place ravioli in freezer. Once ravioli is frozen, remove from tray and place in an airtight container or freezer bag. Freeze until ready to use.

Nutrition (per serving): 137 calories

Saturated Fat	1g	
Total Fat	7g	(45% of calories)
Protein	6g	(18% of calories)
Carbohydrates	13g	(37% of calories)
Cholesterol	71mg	
Sodium	104mg	

My Notes and Recipe variations

Ravioli with Sun-dried Tomatoes

Serves   8

Preparation   :15   Cook   :30   Stand   :00   Total   :45

A great meatless Ravioli with a different flavor.

Ingredients

RAVIOLI-DOUGH Prepare dough as directed
2   pounds ricotta cheese
2   tablespoons Italian flat-leaf parsley, chopped
2 to 4   tablespoons Romano cheese
2   eggs
salt and pepper, to taste

Bring a saucepan with water to a rolling boil. Place sun dried tomatoes into water for 1 to 2 minutes (until pliable, but not too soft). Remove with slotted spoon, drain and cool. Make Ravioli dough as directed and add ½ of the tomatoes, finely chopped to dough and mix well. Mix dough, remove to table and roll into a rectangle approximately ¼ inch thick and 4 inches wide.

Filling:

Add remaining chopped tomatoes (you can use more than the 4 or 5, if desired for a richer flavor) to ricotta, parsley, salt, pepper, eggs and cheese. Mix well. Place about 1 tablespoon of filling in center of left side of dough strip.

Continue placing filling, about 1½ inches apart down long side of dough. Fold dough over filling and cut between filled pockets. Using a pastry crimper or fork, crimp around all sides of dough to seal. Place on a baking sheets in a single layer and let dry for 1½ hours. Either place in freezer on cooking sheet for 1-2 hours, then place in freezer bags, or cook.

To cook, bring a large pot of water with salt, to a rolling boil. Add Ravioli into boiling water and cook for 5-10 minutes, until Ravioli pop to the top of the water. Remove and drain. Pour favorite sauce over top. This particular Ravioli is great served with a Gorgonzola cheese sauce. (see page 408)

Nutrition (per serving): 221 calories

Saturated Fat	10g
Total Fat	16g (67% of calories)
Protein	15g (27% of calories)
Carbohydrates	4g (7% of calories)
Cholesterol	112mg
Sodium	175mg

My Notes and Recipe variations

Stuffed Shells

Serves   6-8

Preparation   :10   Cook   1:40   Stand   :00   Total   1:50

Pre-make the stuffed shells and freeze. They always are great for a last minute meal or that drop in company.

Ingredients

SPAGHETTI SAUCE-MEATLESS
3	cups ricotta cheese
2	eggs
2	tablespoons fresh parsley, chopped
1	pound pasta shells, extra large
2	tablespoons olive oil

salt and pepper, to taste

Bring large pan of water to a boil. Add olive oil and 1 teaspoon salt. Add large shells. Cook until pliable, but not fully cooked, (they should be soft enough to allow you to stuff) about 6-8 minutes. Drain and rinse with cool water. Place shells back in pan in cool water and leave covered until ready to stuff.

In separate mixing bowl add ricotta, eggs, parsley and salt and pepper. Mix well. Drain shells. Remove one large shell from pan. Using thumb and index finger, open shell. Stuff with Ricotta cheese mixture and let sides slightly fold over cheese mixture (stuff with about 3 tablespoons of cheese mixture). Place shell in a baking dish. Continue stuffing shells and placing in baking dish.

Add tomato sauce over top to cover. As shells bake they will absorb the sauce and finish cooking. Bake in a 350 degree oven for 45 minutes to 1 hour.

You can also make the shells, place on a cookie sheet and freeze. When frozen, place in a freezer bag. Great for last minute quick meals or drop in company

Best best store bought sauce I have found that closely resembles some of our family recipes is Classico®

Nutrition (per serving): 565 calories

Saturated Fat	12g	
Total Fat	24g	(38% of calories)
Protein	26g	(18% of calories)
Carbohydrates	62g	(44% of calories)
Cholesterol	133mg	
Sodium	224mg	

My Notes and Recipe Variations

Pasta

Serves 10

Preparation :20 Cook :10 Stand :00 Total :30

Ingredients

1	large onion, chopped
1	pound fresh mushrooms, chopped
1 to 2	fresh garlic cloves, minced (or garlic powder to taste)
2 to 4	tablespoons fresh dill weed, chopped
2	tablespoons vegetable shortening

bread crumbs
salt and pepper, to taste

Source: Gloria Kuska

Fry onion in a large skillet with vegetable shortening. Wash and chop mushrooms and add mushrooms to the onions and cook on high until all water is absorbed; add garlic and saute (if using garlic powder, omit this step). If still too watery, sprinkle lightly with bread crumbs, just to absorb the liquid. Season with salt, pepper and a sprinkle of garlic powder. Cool. Add chopped fresh dill.

Make Pierogi dough and cut 2 inch squares from the dough. Fill the center of the dough with mushroom mixture (about 1 heaping teaspoon. Pinch together all opposite corners of dough on top (this should resemble a chocolate kiss). Freeze until ready to use.

Cook in salted boiling water until they rise to the top.

You can also use this recipe in the classic Pierogi shape.

Nutrition (per serving): 50 calories

Saturated Fat	0g
Total Fat	3g (50% of calories)
Protein	1g (11% of calories)
Carbohydrates	5g (39% of calories)
Cholesterol	0mg
Sodium	42mg

My Notes and Recipe Variations

Pasta

Kapusta (Cabbage Pierogi)

Serves 6

Preparation :10   Cook :35   Stand :00   Total :45

Ingredients

Make PIEROGI DOUGH # 1 as directed
1	green cabbage, cut head into quarters
3	tablespoons butter
1	small onion
1/2	teaspoon salt
1/8	teaspoon black pepper
1/2	cup dried mushrooms, cut, diced, Optional

Cook cabbage in a pot of salted water until tender. Drain well and cool. In a small skillet, saute the chopped onion with butter until tender. Chop cooled cabbage and place with onions (add mushrooms, if desired). Salt and pepper to taste and mix well.

Place in center of Pierogi dough, seal/crimp as instructed and cook as directed.

Nutrition (per serving): 127 calories

Saturated Fat	4g	
Total Fat	7g	(48% of calories)
Protein	3g	(9% of calories)
Carbohydrates	14g	(43% of calories)
Cholesterol	28mg	
Sodium	321mg	

My Notes and Recipe Variations

Nutrition (per serving): 397 calories

Saturated Fat	1g
Total Fat	3g (7% of calories)
Protein	11g (11% of calories)
Carbohydrates	81g (82% of calories)
Cholesterol	72mg
Sodium	39mg

My Notes and Recipe Variations

Pasta

cook until plums are tender. Reduce heat and cook until water forms a slightly thick syrup. Remove from heat and remove the plums. (You can remove the seeds or leave them in). Place a plum in the center of the Pierogi dough, cover and crimp. Cook as directed above. Remove the Pierogi and place in a serving bowl. Cover with the plum syrup and serve hot or cold.

Nutrition (per serving): 123 calories

Saturated Fat	3g
Total Fat	5g (34% of calories)
Protein	1g (5% of calories)
Carbohydrates	19g (62% of calories)
Cholesterol	23mg
Sodium	95mg

My Notes and Recipe variations

Pasta

Pierogi-Potato Filling

Serves 30

Preparation :10 Cook :40 Stand :00 Total :50

Ingredients

8	large white potatoes, peeled and cubed.
2	tablespoons butter
3 to 4	tablespoons milk
1	small onion, chopped

pepper, to taste

Boil potatoes in salted water until soft. Drain well and mash the potatoes with the 1 to 2 tablespoons butter and milk until firm, but smooth. In a medium to large skillet, add remaining butter and melt. Saute the finely chopped onion in the butter until tender.

Add the onion mixture to the mashed potatoes and sprinkle with pepper. Mix and cool. Spoon into Pierogi dough.

My Notes and Recipe variations

Pasta

Nutrition (per serving): 32 calories

Saturated Fat	0g	
Total Fat	1g	(30% of calories)
Protein	1g	(12% of calories)
Carbohydrates	5g	(58% of calories)
Cholesterol	0mg	
Sodium	934mg	

My Notes and Recipe variations

Pasta

Nutrition (per serving): 155 calories

Saturated Fat	6g
Total Fat	12g (70% of calories)
Protein	7g (17% of calories)
Carbohydrates	5g (12% of calories)
Cholesterol	49mg
Sodium	358mg

My Notes and Recipe Variations

Pasta

5. Sauerkraut and mashed potatoes 6. Sauerkraut and mushroom

Nutrition (per serving): 190 calories

Saturated Fat	2g	
Total Fat	4g	(19% of calories)
Protein	6g	(14% of calories)
Carbohydrates	32g	(68% of calories)
Cholesterol	76mg	
Sodium	237mg	

My Notes and Recipe Variations

_____
_____
_____
_____
_____
_____
_____
_____
_____
_____
_____
_____
_____
_____
_____
_____
_____
_____

Pasta

Pierogi Dough-2 (Ciasto Pierogi)

Serves 50

Preparation :15 Cook :20 Stand 1:00 Total 1:35

This recipe was given to me by my dear friend Gloria. This was her mother's, my Auntie Dolores' recipe. We never do anything in a small way. As you will note, recipes will vary from region to region. Simply reduce ingredients proportionately to make fewer Pierogi

Ingredients

10	cups unbleached flour
2	eggs
1½	tablespoons oil
3⅔	cups warm water

Source: Gloria Kuska

Mix together flour, eggs and oil. Begin adding the warm water and mix well until soft and pliable. Knead on the table until the dough is smooth. Using a rolling pin, roll dough into 3 inch by 15 or 20 inch pieces (or use a pasta machine roll first on #1 setting, then re-roll on #3 or 4).

Place filling about 1 inch from edge and place about 1 to 1½ inches apart, along the entire piece of dough. (Fill the center of ½ of the dough strip with about 1 heaping teaspoon of filling). Fold the dough (from long end) over the filling and cut with a cutter or glass. Seal the edges with a fork tine or crimper. Bring a large pan with salt to a boil. Place several Pierogi in pan and let cook for one or two good rolling boils. Remove the Pierogi with a slotted spoon and place in a bowl of cold water. Let sit for 2-3 minutes and remove. Let dry on a towel.

Line the freezer with waxed paper (or place waxed paper on a baking sheet) and place the Pierogi on top of the waxed paper and freeze. (Do not stack Pierogi). Let sit in freezer for ½ hour. Turn Pierogi's over and freeze until completely frozen (about 1 hour). Store in freezer bags, until ready to use.

To serve:

Bring a pan of water to a boil, place Pierogi in water for 2-3 minutes. Remove with slotted spoon. In a large skillet place butter and melt. Blot Pierogi with a towel and place in hot butter, brown on all sides. Remove from skillet and cook remaining Pierogi. To serve, add a little more butter to the skillet, and add bread crumbs, which will absorb the butter Spoon mixture over the top of the Pierogi and serve.

Nutrition (per serving): 95 calories

Saturated Fat	0g
Total Fat	1g (8% of calories)
Protein	3g (12% of calories)
Carbohydrates	19g (80% of calories)
Cholesterol	9mg
Sodium	3mg

My Notes and Recipe variations

Pasta

Serves   6

Preparation   :30   Cook   :15   Stand   :05   Total   :50

Pierogi can be made as a great side dish, a main meal or even a dessert.

Ingredients

4	cups unbleached flour, sifted
4	eggs
8	ounces sour cream
½	teaspoon salt

To a large bowl add sifted flour. Make a well in the center and add eggs, sour cream and salt. Mix well. Remove dough from bowl and place on a lightly floured surface (dough will be somewhat stiff). Knead the dough for 5 minutes. Roll out the dough into ⅛ inch thickness. Cut out circles using a 5 inch round cutter Fill with favorite filling (sauerkraut, mashed potato, plums, etc.).

Brush edges of dough with a little egg white to help hold together. Fold dough over filling to make ends meet. Press edges together using your thumb or a fork.

For larger Pierogi's, after rolling out dough lightly press a glass or cookie cutter onto dough to give you guidance in filling dough (do not cut all the way through). Place filling in center of circle. Place another rolled layer of dough over the top.

Using cutter, center over each filled section and press down firmly to crimp and cut. Place on flat surface and allow each Pierogi to dry for about 1½ hours.

To cook:

Bring a pot of salted water to a boil. Reduce heat to simmer. Place Pierogi in simmering water for about 5 minutes Remove from water. In a skillet, brown butter with a little diced onion (optional). Place Pierogi in melted butter and onion mixture. Brown until lightly golden. Serve with sour cream.

Nutrition (per serving): 427 calories

Saturated Fat	4g
Total Fat	12g (25% of calories)
Protein	14g (13% of calories)
Carbohydrates	66g (62% of calories)
Cholesterol	156mg
Sodium	255mg

My Notes and Recipe variations

Pasta

Pierozki y Serem (Small Lazy Dumplings with cheese)

Serves   4

Preparation   :45   Cook   :15   Stand   :00   Total   1:00

Ingredients

2	cups Farmers Chees or Cottage cheese
1	tablespoon butter (softened)
4	eggs, separate yolks from whites
½	teaspoon salt
1	cup sugar
½	cup unbleached flour

Strain cottage cheese through rise masher or sieve. Add butter and 4 yolks, salt, sugar and flour. In separate bowl, lightly beat egg whites until frothy. Add beaten egg whites to cheese mixture. Mix well. When all ingredients are thoroughly mixed, turn out dough onto a lightly floured surface. Separate dough into 2 pieces. Roll dough into loaf shape (about 2 inch in diameter). Using thread, lay thread underneath dough loaf. Pull both ends over the dough and gently cross to cut the dough into ½ inch pieces.

Bring a large pot of water (with ½ teaspoon salt) to a simmer. Drop dumplings into simmering water until cooked (about 5 minutes) When dumplings are cooked, serve with favorite meal.

Nutrition (per serving): 468 calories

Saturated Fat	7g
Total Fat	13g (25% of calories)
Protein	22g (19% of calories)
carbohydrates	65g (56% of calories)
Cholesterol	237mg
Sodium	847mg

My Notes and Recipe variations

Pasta

Salads and Vegetables

Bean Salad-Creamy

Serves 10

Preparation :10   Cook :00   Stand 3:00   Total 3:10

Growing up, picnics just wouldn't be the same without Grandma and Mom's bean salad.

Ingredients

3	16 oz. cans red kidney beans, drained and rinsed
1-2	dill pickles, large (new dill or half sour) or 2-3 medium, diced
6	celery stalks, diced
1	small green bell pepper, diced
½	cup mayonnaise, (or sour cream) more may be added, if needed

salt, and pepper to taste

Open, drain and rinse kidney beans in a colander. Place beans in bowl. Add diced pickle and celery. Stir gently. Add mayonnaise (or sour cream) and mix. (You may wish to try ½ mayonnaise and ½ sour cream for a special flavor.) You may wish to try celery salt instead of regular salt. Add more mayonnaise if need be.

Nutrition (per serving): 205 calories

Saturated Fat	2g	
Total Fat	9g	(41% of calories)
Protein	7g	(14% of calories)
Carbohydrates	23g	(44% of calories)
Cholesterol	4mg	
Sodium	671mg	

My Notes and Recipe variations

_____
_____
_____
_____
_____

Corn Salad

Preparation   :15   Cook   :00   Stand   3:00   Total   3:15

This recipe is great for hot days, requires no cooking and is enjoyed by all. Great for picnics where refrigeration is not readily available.

Ingredients

3	corn on the cob, fresh, raw
2	7-inch long zucchinis, cubed
2	7-inch long yellow squash, cubed
1	red bell pepper, diced
1	small onion, diced
2	tablespoons extra light olive oil
2	teaspoons tarragon wine vinegar
1	teaspoon salt
1	teaspoon black pepper
1/2	teaspoon oregano
2	fresh garlic cloves, diced
1 to 2	tablespoons granulated sugar, Optional

Remove corn from cob. Place corn, zucchini, squash and onion in a small bowl. Mix well. Add remaining ingredients and mix. Refrigerate for 1 hour or overnight so all flavors can meld.

Nutrition (per serving): 137 calories

Saturated Fat	1g
Total Fat	5g (34% of calories)
Protein	3g (10% of calories)
Carbohydrates	19g (56% of calories)
Cholesterol	0mg
Sodium	398mg

My Notes and Recipe Variations

_____

_____

_____

_____

Salads and vegetables

Caesar Salad

Serves   6

Preparation   :10   Cook   :00   Stand   :10   Total   :20

Ingredients

1	head romaine lettuce
1/4	cup Romano cheese
1	lemon, juiced
1/2	teaspoon Worcestershire sauce
2	fresh garlic cloves, minced
3	anchovy fillets, minced, Optional
1/3	cup extra light olive oil
1	teaspoon salt, Optional
1	teaspoon coarsely ground black pepper
1	egg yolk, Optional
1	cup croutons
1	tablespoon Dijon mustard
3	tablespoons red wine vinegar

Clean romaine and break into bite sized pieces. In a large bowl, add oil, Worcestershire sauce, juice from lemons, garlic and anchovies (optional). Mix well. Add 1 egg yolk (optional). Mix well. Just prior to serving add Romano cheese and mix. Pour over salad and toss. Add garlic, cheese or plain croutons.

Homemade croutons:

Use four slices of day old bread (stuffing bread). Cut crust, then cut each piece into 9 cubes. Lightly spray with vegetable oil on all sides. Optionally, sprinkle a little garlic powder over bread. Place flat on cookie sheet and bake in a 350 degree oven for 10 minutes. Turn over. Cook for several more minutes, until crisp.

Nutrition (per serving): 186 calories

Saturated Fat	3g
Total Fat	16g (76% of calories)
Protein	3g (7% of calories)
Carbohydrates	7g (15% of calories)
Cholesterol	38mg
Sodium	199mg

My Notes and Recipe Variations

Salads and vegetables

Tomato and Basil Salad

Serves   4

Preparation   :10   Cook   :00   Stand   3:00   Total   3:10

Ingredients

4   tomatoes, firm and ripe, cut into wedges
2 to 3   tablespoons fresh basil, chopped
2 to 4   tablespoons light olive oil
1 to 2   tablespoons red wine vinegar
salt and pepper, to taste

Clean tomatoes and cut into wedges. Place all ingredients in a bowl and mix well. Cover and let sit in refrigerator for several hours so all flavors will blend.

Variation: Add some cooked tortellini or cavetelli

Nutrition (per serving): 95 calories

Saturated Fat	1g
Total Fat	7g
Protein	1g (5% of calories)
Carbohydrate	6g (25% of calories)
Cholesterol	0mg
Sodium	108mg

My Notes and Recipe Variations

Cucumber Salad-Vinegar and Dill

Serves 8

Preparation :10 Cook :00 Stand 2:00 Total 2:10

Ingredients

4	cucumbers, washed, etched and sliced
2	tablespoons dill weed
½	cup white vinegar
1	tablespoon light olive oil, Optional
1	teaspoon salt
1	teaspoon pepper

Place all ingredients in a bowl and mix well. Chill for several hours before serving. You can also add chopped onion or tomatoes to this recipe.

Nutrition (per serving): 19 calories

Saturated Fat	0g	
Total Fat	0g	(7% of calories)
Protein	1g	(13% of calories)
Carbohydrates	4g	(80% of calories)
Cholesterol	0mg	
Sodium	297mg	

My Notes and Recipe Variations

Salads and vegetables

Dill Potato Salad

Serves   6

Preparation   :10   Cook   :40   Stand   3:00   Total   3:50

For an added change of flavor, try this potato salad

Ingredients

3	cups potatoes, cooked and sliced
1	cup fresh green beans, blanched
1	small onion, finely diced
1	teaspoon salt
2	tablespoons fresh dill weed, chopped
2	eggs, hard boiled, Optional
1	cup sour cream
2 to 3	tablespoons tarragon vinegar, (or balsamic vinegar)
1/2	cucumber, peeled, diced (or chopped) and drained
1 to 2	fresh garlic cloves, minced or finely diced

In a small to medium mixing bowl, add onion, salt, dill, sour cream, garlic, vinegar and cucumber. Mix well. Cover and chill for at least 1 hour. Place potatoes and green beans (optional) in a large serving bowl (with cover). Pour sour cream mixture over potatoes and mix. Refrigerate for another hour. Add chopped eggs, if desired, and serve.

Nutrition (per serving): 177 calories

Saturated Fat	3g
Total Fat	8g (43% of calories)
Protein	3g (8% of calories)
Carbohydrates	22g (49% of calories)
Cholesterol	15mg
Sodium	471mg

My Notes and Recipe Variations

Salads and vegetables

Mesclun (Mescaline) Salad Greens

Serves 10

Preparation :30   Cook :00   Stand :00   Total :30

Buy the salad greens fresh. Clean and drain well. Mix in a large bag and refrigerate until ready to use. You can get creative and add different types of salad greens. Some grocery stores or orchards carry this already cleaned and mixed.

Ingredients

1	head frise, (light yellow, curly)
1	head arrugula, (red leafy)
2	heads radicchio
10	dandelion greens
1	small head escarole
1	head green leaf lettuce
1	head red leaf lettuce
1	romaine heart

Clean all greens well. Drain. Break into bite sized pieces.

Mix all greens together. Drain well, preferably using a salad spinner. Let sit on a towel until dry. Wrap in paper towel and place in plastic bag until ready to use.

Nutrition (per serving): 42 calories

Saturated Fat	0g	
Total Fat	0g	(10% of calories)
Protein	2g	(23% of calories)
Carbohydrates	7g	(67% of calories)
Cholesterol	0mg	
Sodium	57mg	

My Notes and Recipe variations

Broccoli and Tomatoes

Serves   4

Preparation   :15   Cook   :45   Stand   :00   Total   1:00

A great side dish or served over pasta.

Ingredients

2	fresh garlic cloves, chopped
1/2	teaspoon oregano
1/3	cup dry red wine
1 1/2	pounds tomatoes, peeled and chopped
2 1/2	cups broccoli, chopped (or florets)
1	tablespoon tomato paste
1	teaspoon basil
1	cup chicken broth

salt and pepper, to taste

In a large pot, sprayed with non-stick cooking spray; add onion, garlic, oregano and basil. Saute until tender. Add remaining ingredients EXCEPT broccoli. Stir well. Cover and cook over medium low heat for 30 minutes. During last 5 minutes of cooking, add broccoli, stir, cover and cook until broccoli is tender crisp. Serve as a side dish. This is also great over pasta.

Nutrition (per serving): 76 calories

Saturated Fat	0g	
Total Fat	1g	(13% of calories)
Protein	4g	(20% of calories)
Carbohydrates	13g	(68% of calories)
Cholesterol	0mg	
Sodium	496mg	

My Notes and Recipe Variations

Eggplant and Zucchini Salad

Serves 6

Preparation :15   Cook :20   Stand 8:00   Total 8:35

Ingredients

3	Italian eggplants
3	small zucchinis
6	celery stalks, diced
2	fresh garlic cloves, diced
1	pound plum tomatoes, peeled and chopped with juice
1	cup black olives, pitted and slice (or halved)
4	tablespoons light olive oil
2	tablespoons wine vinegar
2	teaspoons oregano
1	teaspoon basil, chopped
16	oz. can tomato paste

Coarse salt, to remove moisture from eggplant

salt and pepper, to taste

Clean eggplant and zucchini and cut off ends. Cut eggplant and zucchini in half then slice about $\frac{1}{4}$ inch thick. Place eggplant in a colander and sprinkle with salt. Continue layering eggplant and coarse salt until used. Place plate with heavy rock or brick on top of plate and drain for about 1 hour to remove excess moisture. Rinse with cool water to remove excess salt. Place eggplant on a towel, cover and press to remove extra moisture.

In a large skillet add about 2 tablespoons olive oil and heat. Add eggplant and cook until golden (3-5 minutes), turning to lightly brown all sides. Remove eggplant. Add 2 tablespoons more oil and add onion, celery, garlic, tomatoes, tomato paste $\frac{1}{4}$ cup water. Mix well and cook until liquid has evaporated. Remove from skillet and place in bowl to cool. Add olives, parsley, oregano, basil and eggplant. Mix well. Let sit in refrigerator for several hours (or overnight) so all flavors will be absorbed.

Nutrition (per serving): 195 calories

Saturated Fat	2g
Total Fat	12g (57% of calories)
Protein	3g (7% of calories)
Carbohydrates	17g (36% of calories)
Cholesterol	0mg
Sodium	411mg

My Notes and Recipe variations

Salads and vegetables

Nutrition (per serving): 265 calories

Saturated Fat	5g
Total Fat	13g (46% of calories)
Protein	5g (8% of calories)
Carbohydrates	31g (46% of calories)
Cholesterol	15mg
Sodium	767mg

My Notes and Recipe Variations

Salads and Vegetables

Nutrition (per serving): 82 calories

Saturated Fat	1g	
Total Fat	5g	(52% of calories)
Protein	2g	(12% of calories)
Carbohydrates	7g	(36% of calories)
Cholesterol	24mg	
Sodium	57mg	

My Notes and Recipe Variations

Salads and Vegetables

Nutrition (per serving): 105 calories

Saturated Fat	1g
Total Fat	5g (47% of calories)
Protein	2g (9% of calories)
Carbohydrates	12g (44% of calories)
Cholesterol	0mg
Sodium	291mg

My Notes and Recipe Variations

Salads and vegetables

Nutrition (per serving): 157 calories

Saturated Fat	1g
Total Fat	6g (32% of calories)
Protein	2g (6% of calories)
Carbohydrates	24g (62% of calories)
Cholesterol	0mg
Sodium	478mg

My Notes and Recipe Variations

Salads and vegetables

Nutrition (per serving): 396 calories

Saturated Fat	6g
Total Fat	29g (65% of calories)
Protein	4g (4% of calories)
Carbohydrates	30g (31% of calories)
Cholesterol	20mg
Sodium	271mg

My Notes and Recipe Variations

Salads and Vegetables

Nutrition (per serving): 276 calories

Saturated Fat	2g
Total Fat	16g (52% of calories)
Protein	27g (39% of calories)
Carbohydrates	7g (9% of calories)
Cholesterol	396mg
Sodium	76mg

My Notes and Recipe Variations

Salads and Vegetables

Nutrition (per serving): 297 calories

Saturated Fat	4g
Total Fat	28g (84% of calories)
Protein	3g (4% of calories)
Carbohydrates	9g (12% of calories)
Cholesterol	0mg
Sodium	637mg

My Notes and Recipe Variations

Salads and vegetables

Nutrition (per serving): 181 calories

Saturated Fat	4g
Total Fat	9g (46% of calories)
Protein	3g (7% of calories)
Carbohydrates	21g (47% of calories)
Cholesterol	59mg
Sodium	478mg

My Notes and Recipe Variations

Salads and Vegetables

Nutrition (per serving): 131 calories

Saturated Fat	1g	
Total Fat	6g	(38% of calories)
Protein	2g	(6% of calories)
Carbohydrates	18g	(56% of calories)
Cholesterol	0mg	
Sodium	241mg	

My Notes and Recipe Variations

_____
_____
_____
_____
_____
_____
_____
_____
_____
_____
_____
_____
_____
_____
_____

Salads and Vegetables

German Potato Salad

Serves   4

Preparation   :15   Cook   :45   Stand   :00   Total   1:00

Ingredients

3	cups red potatoes, (12 cups = 5 lbs. potatoes)
4	slices bacon, cut and cooked crisp
1	medium sweet onion, chopped
1/4	cup cider vinegar
2	tablespoons water
2	tablespoons sugar, Optional
1	teaspoon salt
1	tablespoon parsley

Source: Aunt Julie Fedor

Wash potatoes (leaving skin on). Cut into bite sized pieces. Cook red potatoes (with skins still on) until tender. In a skillet cook bacon until crisp. Remove bacon and add onion and saute until tender; add bacon and remaining ingredients, stirring well.

Remove from heat. When potatoes are cooked, drain well. To a large bowl, add potatoes and dressing mixture and mix well. Salt and pepper to taste. Serve hot.

Grandma Lil's Cole Slaw

Serves 10

Preparation :20 Cook :10 Stand :00 Total :30

Enjoy this cole slaw on a hot day when you don't want to cook.

Ingredients

1	head cabbage, grate or chop
¼	cup water
¼	cup vinegar
1	egg, beaten
2	slices bacon
1	each medium sweet onion, chopped
1	tablespoon Cannola oil

In a large bowl, beat egg fully. In a pot, add water and vinegar. Bring to a boil. Using a whisk, add the water and vinegar mixture to the beaten egg, very slowly to prevent curdling. Add one tablespoon of Cannola oil to thicken dressing.

In a fry pan (or microwave) fry the bacon until very crisp. Remove from pan and place on paper towel to remove excess grease. Crumble bacon to use in dressing.

In a large bowl, place the grated (or chopped) cabbage. Add the dressing and crumbled bacon. Mix well. Add the chopped onion (as much as you desire) and mix.

Make one day ahead for better flavor.

Green Bean and Tomato Salad

Serves   8

Preparation   :30   Cook   :20   Stand   :00   Total   :50

Great for picnics because continuous refrigeration is not needed.

Ingredients

2	pounds fresh green beans, cleaned and cut into 2 inch pieces
1	large red onion, diced, sliced or chunks
6	Roma tomatoes, cut in eighths
1	tablespoon extra light olive oil
2	tablespoons Cannola oil
1	teaspoon tarragon wine vinegar
1	teaspoon dried oregano
1	teaspoon granulates garlic

Clean and cut green beans into bite sized pieces. You will need to blanch the green beans by placing them in a small colander on top of a pot of boiling water. These should be steamed for several minutes, until the green beans obtain a dark green color, but are still somewhat crisp.

When green beans are blanched, place in a large mixing bowl. Add the chopped or sliced onion and cut tomatoes. In an empty jar, add the olive and Cannola oil, vinegar, oregano and granulated garlic. Shake, then let stand for a few minutes. Pour the dressing onto the beans and tomatoes and mix well. You do not have to use all of the dressing. Just make sure that the salad is coated well. Add salt and pepper to taste.

Italian Potato Salad

Serves 5

Preparation :10 Cook :45 Stand :00 Total :55

Ingredients

10	small red potatoes, about 2 in. in diameter; quartered
1	teaspoon salt
1	teaspoon dried oregano
2 to 3	tablespoons extra light olive oil
1	teaspoon ready-to-use garlic, minced, Optional
1	teaspoon red wine vinegar

Scrub potatoes until clean, do NOT peel. Cut potatoes into quarters (bite sized). Place potatoes in a pot and cover with cold water. Add one teaspoon salt to the water. (Sea salt is healthier to use). Boil potatoes until cooked (about 45 minutes).

To serve hot:

Drain potatoes (save liquid if you want to make a gravy for your meat). Add 1-2 teaspoons olive oil, 1 teaspoon minced, crushed garlic, salt and pepper to taste and sprinkle lightly with oregano (about $1/4$ to $1/2$ teaspoon). Mix well. Serve immediately.

To serve cold:

Drain potatoes. Rinse with cold water to stop the cooking process and cool down the potatoes. Let drain thoroughly. Add olive oil, vinegar, minced, crushed garlic, salt and pepper to taste and oregano; mix well. Place in a sealed container overnight.

Layered Potato Salad

Serves 15

Preparation :10   Cook :45   Stand 24:00   Total 24:55

Ingredients

8	potatoes, boiled and sliced
2	cups mayonnaise
1½	cups sour cream
1½	teaspoons horseradish
1	teaspoon celery seed
½	teaspoon salt
1	cup fresh parsley, chopped
2	medium sweet onions, sliced thin

Source: Merlo Bailey

In a small mixing bowl, add mayonnaise, sour cream, horseradish and celery seed. Mix well. Slice potatoes and onions. Place one layer of potatoes in the bottom of serving dish. Place a layer of the mayonnaise-sour cream mixture then a layer of onion. Sprinkle lightly with parsley. Repeat the process (potato, dressing, onion, parsley) until all ingredients are used. Cover with plastic wrap and refrigerate overnight.

Marinated Calamari Salad

Serves 4

Preparation :10 Cook :10 Stand 24:00 Total 24:20

Ingredients

1½	lbs.. squid, cleaned and sliced ¼ inch thick
1½	cups water
2	green onions, diced
3	fresh garlic cloves, diced
2	tablespoons Italian flat-leaf parsley, chopped
2	teaspoons basil, chopped
¼	cup extra light olive oil
1 to 2	tablespoons tarragon vinegar, (or balsamic)
1	small red onion, thinly sliced
2	stalks kohlrabi, sliced, diced

Buy fresh, cleaned squid and cut into ¼ inch slices. In a medium saucepan, add water, green onions and garlic and bring to a boil. Add the squid and cook for several minutes until tender firm (about 5 minutes). Remove from water with a slotted spoon and place on paper towels to dry and cool.

Once cooled, place squid with remaining ingredients in a salad bowl and mix well, tossing to ensure everything is coated. Add more garlic if desired. For best flavor, chill overnight.

Mushroom Salad-Marinated

Serves   8

Preparation :15   Cook :00   Stand   2:00   Total   2:15

Ingredients

1	cup extra light olive oil, (or salad oil)
2	teaspoons salt
2¹/₂	teaspoons basil, dried
2¹/₂	teaspoons Dijon mustard
¹/₂	teaspoon pepper
¹/₂	teaspoon paprika
6	tablespoons white wine vinegar
4	teaspoons lemon juice
2	pounds mushrooms, sliced (or small button mushrooms whole)
1¹/₂	cups scallions, thinly sliced (including tops)
1 to 2	cups cherry tomatoes, cleaned

Source: Merlo Bailey

In a blender (or in a large jar with lid) add oil, salt, basil, mustard, pepper, paprika, vinegar and lemon juice. Mix well.

Clean mushrooms and slice (or use small button mushrooms whole). Place mushrooms and onions in a large bowl. Pour marinade over, mix well and cover with plastic wrap. Marinade for at least two hours at room temperature. Refrigerate. Just prior to serving, mix in tomatoes and serve.

Red Potato Salad with Mayonnaise

Serves 10

Preparation :15 Cook :45 Stand 2:00 Total 3:00

Ingredients

15	small red potatoes, cut into quarters, bite sized
6	large celery stalks, cleaned and cut into bite size pieces
1	teaspoon fresh dill weed
1	teaspoon salt
1	small sweet onion, diced
1	cup mayonnaise
2	large eggs, diced

Clean potatoes and cut into quarters (bite sized pieces). Add to a pot and fill with water. Boil potatoes for 30-45 minutes until cooked, but still firm. When a fork placed into a potato lifts out easily the potatoes are cooked.

Drain the potatoes (you may wish to save the water and freeze it for using with gravy at a later date). using a colander and rinse with cool water until no longer hot. Thoroughly drain, then place in a large mixing bowl. Chop the celery and add to the potatoes. Add the 1 teaspoon salt and pepper, dill weed (if you want to use dried dill weed you will need to add a little more (about $\frac{1}{4}$ teaspoon, since dried dill tends to have less potency).

Add onion and mix well. Add mayonnaise until thoroughly mixed. (Add more if you like a richer, creamier flavor). Refrigerate for at least 1 hour.

Red Potato Salad-Marinated

Serves 10

Preparation :30 Cook 1:00 Stand :30 Total 2:00

Great for picnics outdoors because this salad does not have to stay as cold as a mayonnaise based salad.

Ingredients

15	small red potatoes, cut and quartered
1	small red onion, cut and diced, Optional
2	tablespoons Cannola oil
2	tablespoons extra light olive oil
1	teaspoon dried oregano
1	teaspoon salt
1	teaspoon garlic powder
1½	teaspoons wine vinegar
2	tablespoons red wine vinegar

Clean and cut the potatoes into quarters. Place in a large pot, fill with water and boil until completely cooked (about 45 minutes or until fork placed into one of the potatoes comes out easily). Thoroughly drain potatoes (you may wish to save the potato water and freeze for use in gravies at a later date) in a colander and rinse with cold water, until cool to the touch. Add potatoes to a bowl. Add remaining ingredients (except vinegar) and stir until well mixed (being careful not to break the potatoes). Add vinegar and mix. Refrigerate for at least 1 hour; preferably overnight so all of the flavors can be absorbed by the potatoes.

Tomato y Mozzarella di bufala

Sliced tomatoes with buffalo mozzarella cheese (or regular mozzarella)

Serves 6

Preparation :15 Cook :00 Stand :15 Total :30

Did you know that true mozzarella is made from buffalo milk, but the U.S. made cheese is generally made from cow's milk. Although this recipe can be made using 'regular' mozzarella, the 'buffalo' cheese is creamier and tastier when eating it as a dish.

Ingredients

6	Roma tomatoes, sliced lengthwise about $1/2$ inch thick
1	lb. mozzarella cheese, cut into 12 slices
$1/4$	cup extra virgin olive oil
1	teaspoon fresh garlic cloves, minced
$1/2$	teaspoon dried oregano

Slice tomatoes. Slice mozzarella cheese into 12 or 24 slices (depending on the diameter of the cheese–it needs to fit on the tomato). In a small jar (with lid) add the olive oil, garlic and oregano. Let stand for 15 minutes. Arrange the tomato and cheese slices on a plate, alternating between them. Pour the oil mixture on each piece as you arrange. Refrigerate for 15 minutes before serving.

Variation:

1. Place a thin slice of prosciutto (Italian ham) on top of tomatoes and cheese

2. Add 1-2 teaspoons tanagon vinegar to dressing.

Tortellini Salad

Serves   8

Preparation   :15   Cook   :20   Stand   3:00   Total   3:35

This is a great recipe for hot days and can be eaten as a meal

Ingredients

2	lbs.. fresh cheese-filled Tortellini
2	cups broccoli florets, blanched
1/4	cup extra virgin olive oil
2	teaspoons ready-to-use garlic, minced
1	teaspoon salt
1	teaspoon black pepper
1	teaspoon dried oregano
114	oz. can pitted black olives

In a jar with lid, add olive oil and minced garlic. Let stand for at least 1 hour (preferably overnight). Cut and clean broccoli so you obtain 2 cups of florets. Blanch or steam slightly so they are tender crisp (when broccoli starts to turn a dark bright green). Drain black olives. Cook cheese Tortellini as directed, drain and rinse with cool water. Drain and let standing for 30-45 minutes. In a large bowl, add Tortellini, broccoli, and olives. Pour oil mixture over and mix until well coated. Add salt and pepper to taste. Leave Tortellini salad in refrigerator for several hours (or overnight) for the best flavor.

Nutrition (per serving): 315 calories

Saturated Fat	11g
Total Fat	26g (73% of calories)
Protein	15g (20% of calories)
Carbohydrates	6g (7% of calories)
Cholesterol	59mg
Sodium	289mg

My Notes and Recipe variations

Salads and vegetables

Nutrition (per serving): 492 calories

Saturated Fat	4g
Total Fat	20g (37% of calories)
Protein	19g (15% of calories)
Carbohydrates	59g (48% of calories)
Cholesterol	54mg
Sodium	1151mg

My Notes and Recipe Variations

Salads and Vegetables

Aunt Vi's Eggplant in Olive Oil

Serves 10

Preparation :20 Cook :00 Stand 72:00 Total 72:20

Aunt Vi and Grandma always made the best eggplant. This eggplant is great served as a side dish or on a sandwich. Although this takes several days to make, it is well worth the wait.

Ingredients

4	eggplants, heavy, no blemished, uniformly dark purple, not wrinkled
1	tablespoon crushed red pepper, (more or less as desired), Optional
2	cups extra light olive oil, to cover eggplant for storage (more may be needed)
6 to 10	fresh garlic cloves, diced
2	teaspoons dried oregano, Optional

Coarse sea salt, to sprinkle over eggplant to remove moisture

Wash (or rinse) eggplant. Cut off ends. Cut each eggplant in $\frac{1}{4}$ inch slices. Place one layer of eggplant in a colander. Cover with coarse salt, place another layer of eggplant and generously cover with salt. Continue this layering process until all eggplant is coated with salt. Place a plate on top of eggplant (slightly smaller than circumference of colander to ensure the plate is touching the eggplant. Place a large (clean) rock or brick (or use a large unopened can of tomatoes) on top of plate. This will act as a weight to help squeeze out excess moisture. Let sit in a dry place for several days, until moisture is removed. Make sure you check the plate or bowl daily and remove any excess water that has accumulated.

In a large clean airtight container place the olive oil, red pepper and chopped garlic. Stir and cover. Let sit until eggplant is ready.

After 3-4 days, lightly rinse the eggplant to remove excess salt. Place plate and brick back on and drain for another 30 minutes to 1 hour. Place eggplant in a large absorbent towel and press down to remove excess moisture. (You may need to use several towels).

You may cut the eggplant into bite sized pieces or use slices whole. Place eggplant in a large bowl, add remaining ingredients and mix well. Place eggplant mixture into mason jars and refrigerator for several days, allowing the eggplant to absorb all of the flavors.

Nutrition (per serving): 404 calories

Saturated Fat	6g
Total Fat	43g (96% of calories)
Protein	1g (1% of calories)
Carbohydrates	3g (3% of calories)
Cholesterol	0mg
Sodium	41mg

My Notes and Recipe variations

Salads and vegetables

Nutrition (per serving): 281 calories

Saturated Fat	3g
Total Fat	8g (25% of calories)
Protein	4g (5% of calories)
Carbohydrates	49g (70% of calories)
Cholesterol	14mg
Sodium	71mg

My Notes and Recipe Variations

Salads and Vegetables

Nutrition (per serving): 298 calories

Saturated Fat	7g	
Total Fat	20g	(61% of calories)
Protein	6g	(9% of calories)
Carbohydrates	22g	(30% of calories)
Cholesterol	23mg	
Sodium	359mg	

My Notes and Recipe variations

Salads and vegetables

Nutrition (per serving): 83 calories

Saturated Fat	1g
Total Fat	2g (18% of calories)
Protein	6g (27% of calories)
Carbohydrates	11g (55% of calories)
Cholesterol	5mg
Sodium	186mg

My Notes and Recipe Variations

Salads and Vegetables

Nutrition (per serving): 170 calories

Saturated Fat	3g
Total Fat	8g (40% of calories)
Protein	4g (10% of calories)
Carbohydrates	22g (51% of calories)
Cholesterol	8mg
Sodium	1096mg

My Notes and Recipe Variations

Salads and Vegetables

Double Baked Potatoes

Serves   4

Preparation   :10   Cook   1:00   Stand   :00   Total   1:10

Ingredients

2	large baking potatoes
2	tablespoons butter
2	tablespoons cream
1	tablespoon Romano cheese

Clean potatoes. Bake potatoes in a 350 to 375 degree oven for 45 minutes to 1 hour, until done. Remove from oven. Cut potatoes in half and scoop out the potato from the skin (retain skin). Put potato pulp in a blender (or use a hand mixer) and add butter, cream and cheese. Whip until light. Divide the potato mixture and spoon into skins. Return to oven and bake an additional 10 minutes until the tops are golden brown and the potato is heated thoroughly.

Nutrition (per serving): 261 calories

Saturated Fat	6g
Total Fat	10g (33% of calories)
Protein	4g (7% of calories)
Carbohydrates	39g (60% of calories)
Cholesterol	29mg
Sodium	77mg

My Notes and Recipe Variations

Salads and vegetables

or rectangular baking dish, place enough sauce in bottom to coat. Place a layer of eggplant on top of sauce. Sprinkle with Romano and grated mozzarella cheese. Add more sauce, eggplant and cheese (depending on the size of the baking dish you can place 2 to 3 layers of eggplant, ending with a sprinkle of mozzarella on top. Bake in a 350 degree preheated oven for 30 minutes, or until cheese is melted and slices are hot.

NOTE:

If you freeze the eggplant (or left over eggplant) for a future date, make sure you thaw the eggplant and blot dry with paper towels before using in the Parmigiana recipe.

Nutrition (per serving): 179 calories

Saturated Fat	1g
Total Fat	2g (12% of calories)
Protein	5g (11% of calories)
Carbohydrates	34g (76% of calories)
Cholesterol	54mg
Sodium	250mg

My Notes and Recipe Variations

Nutrition (per serving): 153 calories

Saturated Fat	3g
Total Fat	5g (32% of calories)
Protein	8g (20% of calories)
Carbohydrates	18g (48% of calories)
Cholesterol	50mg
Sodium	161mg

My Notes and Recipe Variations

Salads and Vegetables

Nutrition (per serving): 156 calories

Saturated Fat	2g
Total Fat	13g (73% of calories)
Protein	3g (7% of calories)
Carbohydrates	8g (20% of calories)
Cholesterol	7mg
Sodium	78mg

My Notes and Recipe Variations

Salads and Vegetables

Black-eyed Beans

Serves   4

Preparation   :10   Cook   3:00   Stand   :00   Total   3:10

Black-eyed beans are a great side dish to pork or chicken. In addition, they make a great main dish, served with rice and a salad.

Ingredients

116	oz. package black-eyed beans
6	slices bacon, (or salt pork)
2	quarts water
1 to 2	teaspoons chili powder
1	teaspoon garlic cloves, minced

salt and pepper

Place beans in a colander and rinse well. Remove any stones or impurities from beans. Add beans to a 5 quart Dutch oven and add 2 quarts of water (8 cups). Bring beans to a boil, then reduce heat to a simmer. Simmer for 1 hour. Add bacon, garlic, salt and pepper, continue to simmer for approximately $1^{1}/_{2}$ to 2 hours, until beans are tender. Serve plain or over white rice.

Variation:
You can add chopped onions and green peppers to the beans approximately 30 minutes before cooking is finished for added flavor.

Polish Style Sauerkraut (Kiszona Kapusta)

Serves 12

Preparation :15 Cook 2:00 Stand :00 Total 2:15

Grandma Catherine use to make this sauerkraut. Our mouths just water thinking about it. This is a personal favorite of mine. Served with Roast Port, dumplings and gravy.

Ingredients

4	pounds Frank's Polish Style Sauerkraut™, two 32 oz. jars, drained, NOT rinsed
$1/3$	pound bacon, cut into $1/4$ inch pieces
1	large onion
2	large Idaho potatoes, grated

In a large pot, add bacon and cook until crisp. Add chopped onion and saute until tender. Add sauerkraut and 2-3 cups of water (just enough to cover the sauerkraut. Cook over high heat for 5-10 minutes, reduce heat to medium and continue cooking until sauerkraut is tender (about 2 to $3^{1}/_{2}$ hours). Add more water as necessary to not dry out. When sauerkraut is tender, grate the potatoes over the pot and stir well. This will thicken the sauerkraut. Continue cooking for another 30-40 minutes on a low to medium heat.

Suggestion:

If you cannot find the Frank's Polish Style Sauerkraut™ (refrigerated section), you may use other 'fresh' kraut found in the refrigerated section of the grocery store. These other brands often are in jars or plastic bags. Make sure there is no sugar in the sauerkraut (unless it is desired).

Eggplant, Breaded

Serves   8

Preparation   :10   Cook   :45   Stand   :00   Total   :55

This same recipe can be used for zucchini. If you are making as a snack, you may wish to cut the eggplant or zucchini into strips.

Sliced and pre-breaded cooked eggplant can be frozen for no more than 2 months, thawed, then used in Parmigiana.

Ingredients

2	eggplants, peeled and cut into $^3/_8$ inch slices
1 to 2	cups arrowroot
2 to 3	eggs, well beaten
2	cups seasoned bread crumbs

sea salt, for draining eggplant

Source: Auntie Mary Jane

Cut off ends of eggplant and peel. Cut into $^3/_8$ inch slices.

Place drained eggplant on paper towels until dry. In separate bowls, place arrowroot, beaten eggs, seasoned bread crumbs. (To make your own seasoned bread crumbs, place 2 cups regular bread crumbs, 2 to 4 tablespoons Romano cheese, $^1/_2$ tsp. garlic powder and 1 tablespoon dried parsley flakes. Mix well).

In a large skillet, place $^1/_3$ to $^1/_4$ cup of Cannola oil and heat on a medium heat. While oil is heating, coat several pieces of eggplant in the arrowroot, covering all sides. Place coated eggplant quickly into eggs and coat, then into seasoned bread crumbs. Place coated eggplant into medium hot oil and lightly brown on all sides. Remove from skillet and place on paper towels to remove excess oil. (I generally use several layers of paper towels, then place the eggplant on paper towels and layer with more paper towels). Continue this practice until all eggplant is cooked. Serve warm or as a snack. If you will freeze for a future use, let cool thoroughly. Layer eggplant between sheets of waxed paper, then wrap in foil, then in a freezer bag. If you wish to make Parmigiana, immediately: Make tomato sauce in a square

Escarole-Wilted

Serves   6

Preparation   :20   Cook   :10   Stand   :00   Total   :30

Ingredients

3	fresh garlic cloves, diced
1/3	cup virgin olive oil
2	pounds escarole, finely chopped (or sliced) (spinach or endive will also work)
1	tablespoon Pecorino Romano cheese
6	slices bacon, (if no bacon is used, increase olive oil to 1/2 cup), Optional
1	teaspoon crushed red pepper, Optional
1	scallion, chopped, Optional

Cut bacon into pieces. Fry bacon in a large skillet, until well cooked. Remove bacon pieces from skillet. Add olive oil, mix and heat. Add garlic, chopped scallion (optional) and crushed red pepper. Saute until tender. Add escarole, a little at a time until wilted, not over cooked (3-5 minutes). Remove from heat, add Romano cheese. Stir well. Serve as a side dish.

Halushki

Serves 6

Preparation :15 Cook :20 Stand :00 Total :35

Ingredients

1	green cabbage, (medium sized, diced into ½ to 1 inch squares)
1	stick butter
3	sweet onions, diced
1	pound package butterfly or bow-tie pasta, cooked according to package directions and drained

salt and pepper, to taste

Cook pasta and drain well. In a large skillet, melt the butter. Add onion and cabbage and mix well. Cook over a low to medium heat for approximately 2 hours. Add the cooked bow ties, cook until pasta is well heated. Mix well. Serve hot.

Variation:

1. Add ½ cup of heavy cream when bow ties are added. Cook until thickened. (Make sure pasta is slightly undercooked, as it will finish cooking with the cream.

2. In a separate skillet, brown 1 to 1½ pounds of lean ground beef. Add beef to cabbage mixture at end when you add the pasta. Heat and serve hot.

Nutrition (per serving): 119 calories

Saturated Fat	0g
Total Fat	1g (4% of calories)
Protein	7g (24% of calories)
Carbohydrates	21g (71% of calories)
Cholesterol	0mg
Sodium	386mg

My Notes and Recipe Variations

Salads and Vegetables

Nutrition (per serving): 173 calories

Saturated Fat	1g
Total Fat	8g (40% of calories)
Protein	5g (10% of calories)
Carbohydrates	22g (50% of calories)
Cholesterol	1mg
Sodium	88mg

My Notes and Recipe variations

Salads and vegetables

Pork Flavored String Beans

Serves   6

Preparation :15   Cook :40   Stand :00   Total :55

A tasteful vegetable and enhancement when served with pork chops, pork roast and sauerkraut with dumplings.

Ingredients

1	pound fresh green beans, cleaned
1	ham hock, small or 8 slices bacon)
2	fresh garlic cloves, diced
1	teaspoon salt
1	teaspoon black pepper

Put green beans in a large pot (you may cut into bite sized pieces or leave whole). Fill pot with water to cover the beans by 2 inches. Add the ham hock or bacon, salt, pepper and garlic. Bring water to a boil, then reduce to a simmer. Cover pot and cook beans until tender (about 30-40 minutes). Serve with pork.

Nutrition (per serving): 110 calories

Saturated Fat	2g	
Total Fat	6g	(49% of calories)
Protein	10g	(37% of calories)
Carbohydrates	4g	(14% of calories)
Cholesterol	47mg	
Sodium	724mg	

My Notes and Recipe variations

Nutrition (per serving): 352 calories

Saturated Fat	2g
Total Fat	14g (35% of calories)
Protein	5g (6% of calories)
Carbohydrates	52g (59% of calories)
Cholesterol	0mg
Sodium	604mg

My Notes and Recipe Variations

Salads and vegetables

Mashed Potatoes with Garlic

Serves   6

Preparation   :10   Cook   :45   Stand   :00   Total   :55

For a great flavor change, make mashed potatoes and add fresh roasted or minced garlic.

Ingredients

3	pounds white potatoes
½	stick butter
1	tablespoon ready-to-use garlic, minced
1	tablespoon fresh parsley, chopped, Optional

salt and pepper, to taste

Clean, peel and cut potato into bite sized pieces. Place potatoes in a large pot and add water to cover. Add 1 teaspoon salt to water. Boil until tender. Drain potatoes (reserving liquid for gravy). Place potatoes back in pot. Add butter, garlic and parsley. Mash thorough until there are no lumps. (We often use a hand mixer to speed up the process). Be careful to not over beat with mixer. Add salt and pepper to taste.

Nutrition (per serving): 257 calories

Saturated Fat	1g
Total Fat	1g (4% of calories)
Protein	6g (9% of calories)
Carbohydrates	56g (87% of calories)
Cholesterol	3mg
Sodium	93mg

My Notes and Recipe Variations

Salads and Vegetables

Mashed Sweet Potatoes

Serves   8

Preparation   :15   Cook   1:10   Stand   :00   Total   1:25

Sweet potatoes are a great compliment to any poultry meal. Whether baked or mashed. For a different flavor, try this sweet concoction.

Ingredients

4	large sweet potatoes
¼	cup butter
¼	cup heavy cream
1	cup mini marshmallows, Optional

Source: Merlo Bailey

Bake the sweet potatoes in a 375 degree oven for 45 minutes to 1 hour (until done). Or you can clean and cut up the sweet potatoes and boil in a pot of water until done.

If baking the potatoes, when cooked, cut them in half length wise and scoop out the potato from the skin. Mash the potatoes with butter and ½ of the cream (use more if needed to make light and fluffy).

If boiling potatoes, drain when done (retain liquid for use in gravy) and follow instructions above for mashing potatoes. If no marshmallows are used, scoop the beaten potato mixture and place even amounts back in the skins. Bake in 350 degree oven for 20-25 minutes.

Suggestions:

If using marshmallows, place potato mixture in a lightly greased (or vegetable sprayed) baking dish and cover the potatoes with the marshmallows. Bake in 350 degree oven until the marshmallows melt and brown slightly. This is a great side dish to be served with chicken or turkey.

Nutrition (per serving): 185 calories

Saturated Fat	5g
Total Fat	9g (43% of calories)
Protein	2g (4% of calories)
Carbohydrates	24g (53% of calories)
Cholesterol	26mg
Sodium	74mg

My Notes and Recipe Variations

Salads and Vegetables

Potato Pancakes *(Ziemniak Nalesnick)*

Serves 10

Preparation :15 Cook :30 Stand :00 Total :45

Ingredients

5	pounds white potatoes, peeled and grated (about 6 cups shredded)
3	large eggs
1	large onion, grated
2 to 3	cups unbleached flour
2	teaspoons salt
1	teaspoon black pepper

Clean and peel potatoes. Using a grater, grate potatoes into a large mixing bowl. Grate 1 large onion into potatoes. Add 3 eggs, salt and pepper. Mix well. Gradually add flour (about $\frac{1}{2}$ cup at a time) and mix well. Continue adding flour until the potato mixture is like a medium-thick batter consistency so you can spread it in pan. (You may need more or less flour).

In a large skillet, fill pan with vegetable oil, about $\frac{1}{8}$ to $\frac{1}{4}$" inch in depth. Heat oil. Using a large spoon, spoon potato mixture into hot grease and flatten (so it resembles a pancake).

You should be able to place 3 or 4 pancakes in the pan. Cook for 1-2 minutes until bottom is golden brown. Turn pancake over, using a fork, and cook other side until golden. Place on a paper towel to remove excess oil. You will need to add additional oil during the cooking process, making sure you always have at least $\frac{1}{8}$" of oil in pan. Serve hot.

NOTE:

Potato mixture may turn slightly brown while sitting ready to cook. This will not harm the potato mixture. Simply stir and spoon mixture onto hot oil.

Serving Suggestions:

Serve with cottage cheese, sour cream or for a sweeter treat, use apple sauce or sugar. Our favorite was with cottage cheese, which had chives added.

Nutrition (per serving): 367 calories

Saturated Fat	1g	
Total Fat	2g	(5% of calories)
Protein	10g	(11% of calories)
Carbohydrates	77g	(84% of calories)
Cholesterol	64mg	
Sodium	508mg	

My Notes and Recipe Variations

Salads and Vegetables

Potatoes Anna

Serves   4

Preparation :10   Cook 1:10   Stand :00   Total 1:20

Ingredients

4	large white potatoes, peeled and sliced to ⅛ to ¼" thick
1	stick butter
1½	cups bread crumbs

salt and pepper, to taste

Melt butter in a small to medium sized baking dish. Add bread crumbs and mix. (Remove about ⅓ of bread crumb mixture). Spread evenly on bottom of dish. Place sliced potatoes over bread crumb mixture. Sprinkle with salt and pepper. Spray with non-stick spray and sprinkle with paprika. Use remaining bread crumb mixture and crumble over top. Bake in a 350 degree oven covered for 30 minutes. Remove foil and continue baking another 30-40 minutes, until potatoes are tender. Serve hot.

Variation:

You may wish to sprinkle ½ to 1 cup of grated cheddar cheese over potatoes for a tangy flavor.

Nutrition (per serving): 513 calories

Saturated Fat	2g
Total Fat	5g (9% of calories)
Protein	13g (10% of calories)
Carbohydrates	105g (82% of calories)
Cholesterol	10mg
Sodium	427mg

My Notes and Recipe variations

Salads and vegetables

Sauteed Eggplant

Serves   4

Preparation   :10   Cook   :20   Stand   :00   Total   :30

Great as a side dish to Italian recipes or meat and poultry.

Ingredients

3	Italian eggplants, sliced about ¼ inch
1	small onion, diced, Optional
2	tablespoons olive oil, (or use non-stick vegetable spray)
1	teaspoon salt
½	teaspoon black pepper
2	Italian flat-leaf parsley, chopped
2	tablespoons Romano cheese, grated, Optional
½	cup water
2	fresh garlic cloves, thinly sliced

Wash eggplant and remove ends. Cut into ¼ inch slices. In a skillet, add olive oil and heat. Add garlic and eggplant and over medium heat, lightly brown on both sides, until tender crisp. Add water and remaining ingredients. Cover and simmer for 10 minutes, until eggplant is tender. Serve with Romano cheese lightly sprinkled on top.

Nutrition (per serving): 88 calories

Saturated Fat	1g	
Total Fat	7g	(70% of calories)
Protein	1g	(4% of calories)
Carbohydrates	6g	(25% of calories)
Cholesterol	0mg	
Sodium	591mg	

My Notes and Recipe Variations

Salads and Vegetables

Spinacio y Figiuolo (Spinach and Beans)

Serves   6

Preparation   :15   Cook   1:00   Stand   :00   Total   1:15

Great as a vegetable side dish. Also try this recipe using small Italian pasta, in place of the beans.

Ingredients

2	fresh garlic cloves, finely chopped
1/2	teaspoon salt
1/2	teaspoon black pepper
2	tablespoons extra virgin olive oil
1	2 pound fresh spinach, (or 3 to 4 10 oz packages frozen)
1	16 oz. can white beans, drained and rinsed

Clean spinach well (or open spinach packages). In a large pot, add olive oil and saute garlic until tender. If using fresh spinach, add spinach to pot, then add water to cover spinach Bring to boil, then reduce heat to simmer. Cook spinach until al dante (tender). Water will reduce as spinach cooks and the water evaporates. Add beans at end and cook 10 minutes, until heated thoroughly. Serve as a side dish or as a hearty meal with Italian bread and butter.

If using frozen spinach, add spinach to the pot with 1-2 cups water. Add 1 tablespoon of olive oil and cover. Simmer over low to medium heat, until spinach thaws and is hot. Add beans and cook uncovered for another 10 minutes. Serve warm.

Nutrition (per serving): 195 calories

Saturated Fat	1g
Total Fat	6g (25% of calories)
Protein	11g (23% of calories)
Carbohydrates	25g (52% of calories)
Cholesterol	0mg
Sodium	495mg

My Notes and Recipe Variations

Salads and Vegetables

Squash Medley

Serves   4

Preparation   :10   Cook   :30   Stand   :00   Total   :40

This recipe is ideal for the grill as well as for the oven.

Ingredients

2	zucchini
2	yellow squash
1	medium sweet onion
2	tablespoons butter
10	fresh mushrooms, cleaned and sliced
1	teaspoon dill weed

Clean zucchini and squash. Cut off ends, then cut into slices or cubes. Peel, cut and dice onions. Clean mushrooms and slice. Using aluminum foil tear off a large sheet. Place all ingredients in center. Dab with butter. Place on a rack on grill, or in oven. Bake at 350 degrees (medium heat) for 20-30 minutes, until vegetables are tender, yet crisp.

Nutrition (per serving): 120 calories

Saturated Fat	4g	
Total Fat	6g	(47% of calories)
Protein	3g	(11% of calories)
Carbohydrates	13g	(42% of calories)
Cholesterol	16mg	
Sodium	66mg	

My Notes and Recipe variations

Steamed Asparagus

Serves   4

Preparation   :05   Cook   :10   Stand   :00   Total   :15

Steamed asparagus is great served with a splash of lemon juice, lemon butter or a hollandaise sauce.

Ingredients

1	pound asparagus
¼	cup butter, melted
2 to 4	tablespoons lemon juice

Clean asparagus by cutting or breaking off the end of the stalk where it is too tough to eat. Place the asparagus in a steamer, or colander over a 3-5 quart pot of water (about 1 inch of water).

Bring water to a boil, place asparagus in steamer or colander and place over boiling water and cover. Steam for 6-8 minutes, until asparagus is tender. Salt and pepper as desired and serve with fresh lemon juice squeezed over top. You can also make a lemon butter and pour over top. Melt ¼ cup of butter with 2 to 4 tablespoons of lemon juice. Pour over asparagus.

Nutrition (per serving): 143 calories

Saturated Fat	7g	
Total Fat	12g	(74% of calories)
Protein	4g	(11% of calories)
Carbohydrates	5g	(15% of calories)
Cholesterol	31mg	
Sodium	127mg	

My Notes and Recipe Variations

Stuffed Eggplant with Cheese

Serves 4

Preparation :10 Cook 1:20 Stand :00 Total 1:30

The eggplants you use for this recipe should be about 4 to 6 inches long.

Ingredients

SPAGHETTI SAUCE - MEATLESS Plus

4	Italian eggplants, about 2 fi" to 3" diameter (or regular eggplant)
1	cup ricotta cheese, (you may use a little more if the eggplants are larger)
1	egg
1	teaspoon parsley
½	teaspoon salt
½	teaspoon black pepper
1	tablespoon Romano cheese, grated

Cut off top and bottom from eggplant. (If you desire, peel the eggplant, although this is not necessary, since cooking will soften the skin). Boil a large pot of water, and reduce to a simmer. Gently simmer the eggplants in water until tender and pliable, but not overly soft. (about 15-20 minutes). Remove eggplant from water, and let cool to warm. Carefully make a slit lengthwise down the eggplant to the center and GENTLY begin to open. Scoop out pulp.

In a large mixing bowl add the remaining ingredients and the pulp. Mix well with whisk or on low with a hand mixer. Place some spaghetti sauce in the bottom of a square baking dish. Stuff eggplants with cheese mixture and place, slit side down in a baking dish. Add spaghetti sauce to the top. Bake in a 350 degree oven for 1 hour. Serve with a salad, or with a side dish of pasta.

Nutrition (per serving): 178 calories

Saturated Fat	6g
Total Fat	10g (53% of calories)
Protein	10g (23% of calories)
Carbohydrates	11g (24% of calories)
Cholesterol	86mg
Sodium	425mg

My Notes and Recipe Variations

Salads and Vegetables

Serves   4

Preparation :10   Cook 1:20   Stand :00   Total 1:30

Ingredients

SPAGHETTI or Marinara SAUCE - MEATLESS Plus

4	Italian eggplants, about 2" to 3" diameter (or regular eggplant
1/2	cup Italian flat-leaf parsley, chopped
1/2	teaspoon salt
1/2	teaspoon black pepper
1	tablespoon Romano cheese, grated
1	7-inch long yellow squash, cubed
1	7-inch long zucchini, cubed
4	large tomatoes, peeled
1/2	cup onions, finely chopped
1	tablespoon dill
1/2	cup cooked rice, (slightly under cooked)
2 1/2	MARINARA SAUCE
1/2	cup mushrooms, chopped

Cut off top and bottom from eggplant. (If you desire, peel the eggplant, although this is not necessary, since cooking will soften the skin). Boil a large pot of water, and reduce to a simmer. Gently simmer the eggplants in water until tender and pliable, but not overly soft. (about 15-20 minutes). Remove eggplant from water, and let cool to warm. Carefully make a slit lengthwise down the eggplant to the center and GENTLY begin to open. Scoop out pulp and save.

In a skillet, saute onions in olive oil. Add tomatoes, mushrooms, and 1/2 of eggplant pulp and cook until liquid evaporates. Add zucchini, squash, spices and parsley. Saute an additional 5 minutes until zucchini and squash are tender, yet crisp. Remove from heat. Add remaining ingredients and remaining pulp. Mix well. Place 1/2 cup Marinara sauce and 1/2 cup water in the bottom of a square baking dish. Mix well. Stuff eggplants with vegetable mixture and place, slit side down in a baking dish. Add sauce to the top. (Add a little more water, if need be so sauce is about $1/2$ up side of eggplant). Cover baking dish. Bake in a 350 degree oven for one hour. Serve with a salad, or with a side dish of pasta.

Nutrition (per serving): 275 calories

Saturated Fat	1g	
Total Fat	6g	(20% of calories)
Protein	9g	(13% of calories)
Carbohydrates	46g	(68% of calories)
Cholesterol	1mg	
Sodium	780mg	

My Notes and Recipe Variations

Salads and Vegetables

Zucchini Flower Fritters

Serves   4

Preparation   :10   Cook   :10   Stand   :00   Total   :20

These were a special treat in my Aunt Vi's home.

Ingredients

6 to 10	zucchini, with flowers
2	eggs, well beaten
1	cup unbleached flour
1	cup cold water
2 to 3	cups vegetable oil, (more as needed for deep frying)

Source: Aunt Vi

Break flowers off of the zucchini. Gently remove stem, leaving flower in tact. Gently clean flower and wash skin of zucchini. Cut zucchini on an angle into $1/4$ inch slices.

In a deep fryer or 2 quart saucepan, add oil and heat. While oil is heating, mix egg, water and flour to form a light batter. When oil is heated, dip zucchini pieces in egg batter and gently place in oil. Deep fry for several minutes until golden. Dip flower in egg mixture and gently place in oil to deep fry until golden. Serve hot.

Variation:

The zucchini flowers are very tender and add a nice flavor to eggs. Instead of deep frying the flowers, you can make an egg patty, which can be eaten hot or cold. Beat 3 eggs with about $1/4$ cup of heavy cream. Using a metal egg mold, place in a non-stick skillet, lightly coated with melted butter. Dip the flower in the egg mixture and place in the egg mold. Spoon an extra tablespoon of egg over flower.

Cook until egg is set, turn over and finish cooking (about

2-3 minutes). Remove from pan and place on paper towel to drain. Serve hot or cold.

Nutrition (per serving): 1169 calories

Saturated Fat	14g
Total Fat	112g (86% of calories)
Protein	9g (3% of calories)
Carbohydrates	31g (10% of calories)
Cholesterol	1106mg
Sodium	39mg

My Notes and Recipe variations

Salads and vegetables

Vegetarian Sufretta (Meatless Meatballs)

Serves 6

Preparation :30 Cook 1:10 Stand :05 Total 1:45

Sufretta is an economical way to extend your pasta meal and because it is cooked directly in your spaghetti sauce, it tastes surprisingly like meatballs. Try making the Sufretta and mixing Sufretta with regular meatballs—see who can tell the difference.

Ingredients

2	eggs
¼	cup Romano cheese, grated
2	teaspoons ready-to-use garlic, chopped
½	teaspoon salt
½	teaspoon black pepper
2	teaspoons dried parsley
2	cups bread crumbs
¼	cup water
2	tablespoons instant dried onion, Optional

In large mixing bowl, add eggs and beat well. Add water, garlic, salt, pepper, onions (optional) and parsley. Mix well. Add bread crumbs. Mix well. Let stand 5 minutes. Shape Sufretta into ball shapes or 6 patties. In a large skillet, heat 2 tablespoons olive oil. Add balls or patties and lightly brown on all sides. Remove from pan and place in spaghetti sauce. Cook with sauce for 45 minutes to 1 hour.

Nutrition (per serving): 170 calories

Saturated Fat	1g
Total Fat	4g (22% of calories)
Protein	8g (18% of calories)
Carbohydrates	26g (60% of calories)
Cholesterol	76mg
Sodium	503mg

My Notes and Recipe variations

Salads and vegetables

Soups, Sauces,
Side Dishes, and
Other Tasty Stuff

p.riccio

Fried Rice

Serves   6

Preparation   :20   Cook   :40   Stand   :00   Total   1:00

The basic fried rice recipe below can be modified for individual taste. Try using chicken or shrimp in place of pork. You can also use crisp June peas.

Ingredients

1½	cups long grain rice, raw Hohoko
2¼	cups water
3	eggs
¼	teaspoon salt
½	tablespoon water
2	tablespoons oil
3	scallions, cut into ¼ to ½ inch pieces
2	tablespoons soy sauce
½ to 1	cup pork, Chinese style roasted pork, diced
1	cup fresh bean sprouts
½	cup medium sweet onion, diced

Place rice in a strainer and run cool water over it, stirring to allow excess starch to be removed. Place rice in a bowl with water and continue washing and rinsing until water becomes clear. This will reduce the starch and make a fluffier rice.

Place the cleaned rice in a large saucepan and add 2¼ to 2½ cups of water. Bring to a boil over a medium high heat, stirring occasionally until most of the water has been absorbed. Cover the pan and reduce heat to simmering. Continue cooking for about 20 minutes, until the rice is dry and fluffy.

After rice is cooked, separate with a fork. Lightly beat the eggs with salt and water. Using a wok or cast iron skillet, heat the oil. Add the scallions and onions and stir fry for 1 minute. Add the rice and stir fry until rice is well coated with oil. Slowly pour in egg mixture and continuously stir until eggs are almost set. Add the pork, soy sauce and bean sprouts and stir fry until well mixed. Serve immediately.

Nutrition (per serving): 231 calories

Saturated Fat	1g
Total Fat	8g (31% of calories)
Protein	7g (11% of calories)
Carbohydrates	33g (58% of calories)
Cholesterol	114mg
Sodium	485mg

My Notes and Recipe variations

Serves   8

Preparation   :10   Cook   :45   Stand   :00   Total   :55

This is an excellent side dish to pork or chicken. Can also be used for a main course, if serving other green vegetable or salad for a light lunch.

Ingredients

1	cup rice, short grain, raw
¾	cup water
¾ to 1	cup chicken broth
½	teaspoon salt
1	green bell pepper, finely diced
2 to 3	scallions, finely diced, Optional
½	cup celery, finely diced
2	fresh garlic cloves, finely diced
½	cup peas, fresh or frozen and thawed
½	cup broccoli, chopped
½ to 1	cup cheddar cheese
1	cup milk

salt and pepper, to taste

Place water, chicken broth, and salt in a medium saucepan (one with a lid, preferably a non-stick surface). Stir well and bring to a boil. Add garlic and rice, while gently stirring. Cover the pot and cook over low to medium heat. White rice will take 20-30 minutes depending on the type of rice. Watch rice carefully.

During the last 5-10 minutes of cooking, add celery, bell pepper, peas and broccoli. Stir and continue simmering, uncovered for the remaining time. Remove from heat, and cover. In a separate saucepan (or top of a double boiler), add milk and cheddar cheese. Mix well and heat on low to medium, until cheese melts and milk is hot.

The rice should appear a little dry. Add milk and cheese mixture to rice and stir over low heat. Let sit for 5-10 minutes until rice becomes soft and absorbs the milk and cheese mixture.

Substitutions:

1. Use black beans instead and add some red bell pepper or crushed red pepper for a little spice. If you will use dried red beans, follow package directions for soaking and cooking, then add to the recipe.

Nutrition (per serving): 149 calories

Saturated Fat	2g
Total Fat	4g (22% of calories)
Protein	5g (14% of calories)
Carbohydrates	24g (63% of calories)
Cholesterol	12mg
Sodium	400mg

My Notes and Recipe Variations

Soups, Side Dishes, and Other Tasty Stuff

Mushroom Arborio Rice

Serves 4

Preparation :10 Cook :45 Stand :10 Total :65

Use Arborio rice for a richer, nuttier flavor, although regular white or brown rice will do nicely. Try to use regular rice, rather than instant.

Ingredients

2	cups cooked rice, (firm, slightly undercooked)
1 to 2	scallions, chopped (or either ½ teaspoon onion powder or 1 small minced onion)
1	teaspoon ready-to-use garlic, minced or chopped (add more as desired)
1	tablespoon Italian flat-leaf parsley, finely chopped
½	teaspoon thyme, Optional
¼	cup celery, finely chopped (or 1 teaspoon celery salt)
1	cup whole milk, (or cream)
½	cup water
1	tablespoon butter
10	mushrooms, cleaned, sliced or diced large (½ to 1 cup)

In a large pot, add butter and melt. Add scallions, celery, garlic and mushroom and saute until tender. Add ½ cup water cover and simmer for 10 minutes. Add remaining ingredients (EXCEPT rice) in a blender and mix well. Slowly add milk mixture to water and mushrooms. Bring to a slight boil, stirring constantly. Reduce heat to simmer, cover and cook an additional 5-10 minutes. Add rice and cook for another 20-30 minutes over low to medium heat. Cook until rice is tender and mixture has a creamy consistency

Turn off heat. Let stand covered for 5-10 minutes.

If not usiing Arborio rice, you will have to adjust the recipe accordingly since different rices cook at different rates.

Nutrition (per serving): 209 calories

Saturated Fat	3g
Total Fat	5g (23% of calories)
Protein	5g (10% of calories)
Carbohydrates	35g (67% of calories)
Cholesterol	16mg
Sodium	68mg

My Notes and Recipe Variations

Soups, Side Dishes, and Other Tasty Stuff

Spanish Style Rice

Serves   6

Preparation   :15   Cook   :30   Stand   :10   Total   :55

For an easy one dish meal, just add meat (chicken or pork are best). Cut into strips and saute with onions. This is also easy to make in a crock pot. Simply add all ingredients in the crock pot (no need to peel tomatoes, just dice and toss in). Cook on low or medium for 1-2 hours, depending on your schedule

Ingredients

1	large yellow onion, diced
2	green bell peppers, diced
2	tablespoons oil
6 to 8	tomatoes, peeled and diced (retain juice and seeds)
1	teaspoon salt
½	teaspoon pepper
4 to 6	jalapenos, or chilies, diced
1	6 oz. tomato sauce
1	cup rice
2	cups water

Source: Bel Torio

Core tomatoes. Using a 4-6 quart pot, fill half way with water and boil. Slowly add the tomatoes and cook for 2-3 minutes, skins should become loose. Drain and remove tomatoes and peel skins and dice. Using the same pot, add oil and heat. Add remaining ingredients EXCEPT rice. Bring to a boil. Add rice and reduce to a simmer. Cover and let cook for approximately 30 minutes, until rice is tender. Remove from heat and let sit for 5-10 minutes.

Nutrition (per serving): 232 calories

Saturated Fat	0g
Total Fat	6g (21% of calories)
Protein	5g (8% of calories)
Carbohydrates	41g (71% of calories)
Cholesterol	0mg
Sodium	1015mg

My Notes and Recipe Variations

Soups, Side Dishes, and Other Tasty Stuff

Arborio Rice with Onion and Herbs

Serves 4

Preparation :10   Cook :45   Stand :00   Total :55

This is a savory dish made with Arborio rice and poultry stock. Try it as a side dish to pork or chicken

Ingredients

2	cups cooked rice, (rice should be firm, slightly undercooked)
1	cup cream (or whole milk)
1	scallions, chopped (with leaves)
½	teaspoon basil
½	teaspoon thyme, Optional
½	teaspoon rosemary, Optional
1	teaspoon Italian flat-leaf parsley, finely chopped
1	teaspoon ready-to-use garlic, chopped or minced
½	cup chicken broth
½	teaspoon salt
½	teaspoon black pepper

Using a blender, mix all ingredients EXCEPT rice. Place in a saucepan and cook over medium heat for 5 minutes. Reduce heat to simmer. Add rice and mix well. Cover pan and cook additional 25 minutes. Stir rice approximately every 5 minutes or so and continue to cook over a low to medium heat. Turn off heat, let sit for 5-10 minutes, until rice is tender and creamy

Nutrition (per serving): 284 calories

Saturated Fat	9g	
Total Fat	15g	(48% of calories)
Protein	4g	(6% of calories)
Carbohydrates	32g	(46% of calories)
Cholesterol	52mg	
Sodium	499mg	

My Notes and Recipe Variations

Escarole and Bean Soup (Escarole y Fagiuolo)

Serves 4

Preparation :15 Cook :40 Stand :00 Total :55

This is another hearty recipe that can be served as a main dish and is a great budget extender.

Ingredients

1	head escarole, cleaned
2	fresh garlic cloves, diced, minced
2	16 oz. cans chicken broth
4	cups water
1	12 oz. canned black beans, rinsed
2	tablespoons olive oil
1	small onion, diced, Optional

Clean the escarole well. In a large pot, add the olive oil and saute the garlic (and onion if using) until tender. Add chicken broth and water, bring to a boil. Reduce heat to simmer and add escarole. Cook escarole in broth until tender. Add beans and simmer for 10 minutes, until beans are hot. Serve as a side dish, appetizer or as a hearty soup.

Variation:

You can also make the standard chicken soup recipe and use the broth for a fresh and natural meal.

Nutrition (per serving): 202 calories

Saturated Fat	1g
Total Fat	8g (37% of calories)
Protein	9g (18% of calories)
Carbohydrates	23g (45% of calories)
Cholesterol	0mg
Sodium	1588mg

My Notes and Recipe Variations

Barszcz (Beet and Chicken Soup Polish Style)

Serves   6 to 8

Preparation   :15   Cook   1:00   Stand   :00   Total   1:15

Ingredients

4 to 6	meaty chicken pieces
6 to 7	chicken bouillon cubes
2 to 3	fresh garlic cloves, finely chopped (or 1 to 1 teaspoon garlic powder to taste)
2 to 4	celery ribs, cut
2	tablespoons parsley
3 to 4	carrots, thickly sliced
1	medium sweet onion
3	16 oz. cans beets
2 to 3	tablespoons vinegar
1	teaspoon sugar
1/4 to 1/2	cup dried mushrooms
4	beets, fresh

pepper, to taste

Source: Gloria Kuska

Clean and wash the fresh beets. Bake the beets in a 350 degree oven until slightly hard. Remove from oven and refrigerate, overnight. The next day, peel and shred the beets.

Using a 5 quart pot or Dutch oven, place bouillon cubes, chicken, garlic, celery, parsley, carrots and onions in the pot. Cover with water (3-4 quarts or 12-16 cups). Bring to a boil, reduce heat to medium and continue cooking until chicken falls from bones and vegetables are very tender. Add the 3 cans of beets along with their liquid. Boil gently to blend the flavors. Add vinegar, spoon by spoon and mix well. Add 1 teaspoon sugar and pepper to taste. Mix. Strain soup. Add shredded beets and cooked dried mushrooms to the broth. Top with fresh dill. Serve the vegetables and chicken on the side.

Nutrition (per serving): 375 calories

Saturated Fat	3g
Total Fat	10g (23% of calories)
Protein	19g (20% of calories)
Carbohydrates	53g (57% of calories)
Cholesterol	52mg
Sodium	1683mg

My Notes and Recipe Variations

Soups, Side Dishes, and Other Tasty Stuff

Cabbage Soup

Serves   8

Preparation   :15   Cook   2:10   Stand   :00   Total   2:25

A great beginning for pork or brisket meals that is easy to make.

Ingredients

1	pound boneless beef briskets, (or smoked butt)
2	cups onions, thinly sliced
1½	pounds green cabbage (or white cabbage) cleaned and shredded
½	cup celery, finely diced
1	pound white potatoes, peeled and cut into bite sized pieces
4	tomatoes, peeled and chopped
1	teaspoon salt
1	teaspoon black pepper

In a large pot, add brisket or butt and 12-16 cups of water. Bring to a boil and scrape off any scum that rises to surface. Simmer for 1 to 1½ hours until the meat is very tender. Remove the meat and slice for a side serving. Keep meat stock in pot for use in soup. In a skillet, add butter (or oil) and saute onion until tender. Add cabbage and celery. Cover and simmer over low heat for 10-15 minutes. Add the cabbage mixture to the meat stock. Simmer for ½ hour. Add potatoes and cook for 15 minutes. Add chopped tomatoes (optional) and cook 10 minutes. Serve hot.

Nutrition (per serving): 292 calories

Saturated Fat	6 g	
Total Fat	16g	(48% of calories)
Protein	13g	(18% of calories)
Carbohydrates	25g	(34% of calories)
Cholesterol	41 mg	
Sodium	363mg	

My Notes and Recipe Variations

Soups, Side Dishes, and Other Tasty Stuff

Cabbage and Beef Soup

Serves 8

Preparation :15   Cook   1:10   Stand   :00   Total   1:25

Ingredients

1	pound lean ground beef
½	teaspoon garlic salt
¼	teaspoon pepper
½	head cabbage, chopped
1	28 oz. can canned tomatoes, chopped
1	28 oz. can water
2	pieces celery, chopped
1	16 oz. can kidney beans
4	bouillon cubes, beef
¼	teaspoon garlic powder

parsley, to garnish soup

Source: Auntie Julie

In a large pot or Dutch oven (4 to 5 quart size), add ground beef. Saute until browned. For lower fat recipe, drain beef when browned and ready to pot. Add garlic, pepper, celery and bouillon cubes and mix well. Add water and make sure that the bouillon cubes are fully dissolved. Add tomatoes and cabbage. Bring to a boil. Reduce heat and simmer covered for 45 minutes. Add kidney beans (drained and rinsed) and continue simmering for an additional 15 minutes.

Place soup in bowls and garnish with parsley.

Nutrition (per serving): 424 calories

Saturated Fat	5g
Total Fat	13g (27% of calories)
Protein	27g (26% of calories)
Carbohydrates	50g (47% of calories)
Cholesterol	43mg
Sodium	855mg

My Notes and Recipe Variations

Soups, Side Dishes, and Other Tasty Stuff

Chicken Soup with Homemade Noodles

Serves 10

Preparation :30 Cook 1:30 Stand :00 Total 2:00

You don't have to be a whiz kid in the kitchen to make this soup or noodles, nor do you need all the fancy gadgets. You can also use turkey instead of chicken for a different flavor. A great recipe to use after the Thanksgiving holidays if you are trying to figure out what to do with the leftovers and carcass.

Ingredients

2	skinless boneless chicken breasts
2	skinless chicken thighs
2	chicken leg
5	stalks large celery stalks, cleaned and cut
5	large carrots, sliced
1	teaspoon salt
2	cups unbleached flour
2	large eggs, beaten
1	teaspoon salt
1	teaspoon finely ground black pepper
1	small whole onion, peeled

In a large pot add chicken piece and at least 5 quarts of water. Add 1 teaspoon salt, pepper, celery, and whole onion. Cook for approximately 1 hour on medium to high heat. When chicken is cooked, strain meat and celery through a colander into another pot. Put the stock back on the heat and add the carrots. While carrots are cooking you will make the noodles.

In a large bowl add 2 cups flour, 1 teaspoon salt and stir. Add 2 beaten eggs to the flour mixture (or ½ cup Egg Beater's). Mix thoroughly. The dough will be very stiff, keep working the dough until all of the eggs are blended in.

Turn the dough onto a lightly floured surface. Knead well. Using a rolling pin, roll out the dough into a circular pattern as thin as possible. It may be easier to divide the dough into 2 parts. When the dough is rolled as thin as possible, use a butter knife to cut ¼ inch strips. When all of the dough is rolled and cut, lightly dust the pasta with flour to prevent sticking. Place these strips of pasta into the hot soup. The pasta will only take a few minutes to cook. Serve hot. (You can also use a pasta machine to speed up the process).

Suggestion:

Debone the chicken and return to soup or lightly broil the chicken and serve on the side.

Nutrition (per serving): 209 calories

Saturated Fat	1g
Total Fat	3g (13% of calories)
Protein	21g (40% of calories)
Carbohydrates	25g (48% of calories)
Cholesterol	91mg
Sodium	578mg

My Notes and Recipe Variations

Italian Style Chicken Soup

Serves 10

Preparation :30 Cook 1:00 Stand :00 Total 1:30

In the Italian household, we often made chicken soup, removed the chicken and baked it. Serving the soup only with noodles and the chicken as the entree.

Ingredients

1	whole broiler-fryer chicken
1	16 oz. can tomato sauce
5	stalks celery, cleaned and cut
1	turnip, Optional
4	carrots, cleaned and sliced
1	package assorted fresh vegetables, Optional
1	cup tiny soup pasta
1	each small onion, quartered

Source: Aunt Jeannie

In large pot add whole fryer chicken (less fat). Cover the chicken with water until the water is at least 2 inches above the chicken. Add celery stalks (cut in half). Cook or boil chicken for ½ hour. Lower heat to medium and on a high simmer continue cooking chicken As chicken cooks you will need to skim the top to remove any sediment and extra fat build up. Cook for at least 1 hour, or until you notice the chicken is beginning to separate from bones.

When chicken is cooked, using a colander, strain the meat and celery from the pot into another pot. Take the soup and return to heat. Add tomato sauce and vegetables. Bring to a boil and add the pasta. Cook pasta until it is al dante (cooked and slightly firm). Do not overcook the pasta, since reheating will cause it to further cook. For a nice flavor add grated Romano cheese to the soup.

Suggestion:

Pasta recommended: Orzo, Acini, Bows, Elbow Macaroni. After chicken is removed, place on rack in oven and brown.

Nutrition (per serving): 376 calories

Saturated Fat	5g	
Total Fat	17g	(40% of calories)
Protein	25g	(27% of calories)
Carbohydrates	31g	(33% of calories)
Cholesterol	96mg	
Sodium	755mg	

My Notes and Recipe Variations

Soups, Side Dishes, and Other Tasty Stuff

Cream of Broccoli Soup

Serves   6

Preparation   :20   Cook   1:00   Stand   :00   Total   1:20

Wondering what to do with the Broccoli stems? Clean, peel and chop to make this delicious soup.

Ingredients

2	pounds broccoli, stems or stems and florets
1	small onion, chopped
3	cups milk
3	cups water
1	teaspoon salt
1	teaspoon pepper
4	large white potatoes, grated (or chopped in a food processor)

In a large pot add the water, salt, onion, grated potatoes and chopped broccoli stems (reserve florets, if using). Bring to a boil, then reduce heat to medium and cook until broccoli is tender.

Place broccoli mixture in blender and mix well. Return to the pot on a low heat. In a large blender, add milk and flour. Mix well. Slowly add to the broccoli and let simmer until slightly thick. Take 2 cups of broccoli mixture and add to blender. Add florets and blend. Add this mixture back to the soup and continue to simmer (about 30 minutes) until medium thick. You may wish to add grated cheddar cheese for added flavor. (If broccoli soup is not as thick as you would like, you can add 1 to 2 tablespoons of flour with the last batch of soup you place in the blender).

Nutrition (per serving): 360 calories

Saturated Fat	3g
Total Fat	5g (12% of calories)
Protein	14g (15% of calories)
Carbohydrates	65g (73% of calories)
Cholesterol	17mg
Sodium	509mg

My Notes and Recipe Variations

Soups, Side Dishes, and Other Tasty Stuff

Cream of Chicken Soup

Serves   6

Preparation :15 Cook :30 Stand :00 Total :45

Wondering what to do with left over chicken? Here's a hearty answer for cool winter nights or weekends—Cream of Chicken Soup. This is great served as a meal with crusty bread or rich rye bread.

Ingredients

1	tablespoon onions, chopped
2	tablespoons butter
2	tablespoons flour
2	cups chicken broth, canned is fine
$\frac{1}{2}$	cup light cream
$\frac{1}{2}$	teaspoon salt
$\frac{1}{4}$	teaspoon pepper
1 to 2	cups cooked chicken, diced or thinly sliced
1	cup celery, sliced thin or diced

Source: Merlo Bailey

In a 4 quart saucepan, add butter and melt. Add celery and onions and saute until tender (about 5-10 minutes). Add chicken (if using fresh chicken, saute with onions and celery until cooked).

Cook for additional 5 minutes. Blend in flour with a fork or wire whisk. Add broth and mix well. Continue to cook and stir until broth is slightly thickened. Remove from heat and cool slightly (about 15 minutes). Add cream and seasonings and mix well. Return to low heat and heat through. Serve at once.

NOTE: to cut down on dishes and add a fun treat for the entire family, purchase or make 4 to 6" diameter round bread (such as Italian or Rye). Cut the center top and remove the inside bread to use as a bowl. The kids will love this as much as the adults.

Nutrition (per serving): 189 calories

Saturated Fat	7g	
Total Fat	14g	(64% of calories)
Protein	8g	(16% of calories)
Carbohydrates	9g	(20% of calories)
Cholesterol	54mg	
Sodium	762mg	

My Notes and Recipe Variations

Soups, Side Dishes, and Other Tasty Stuff

Fish Soup

Serves   6

Preparation   :10   Cook   :45   Stand   :00   Total   :55

This recipe is also great served with ¼ cup of rice in the bottom of the bowl.

Ingredients

2	tablespoons extra virgin olive oil
2	tablespoons Italian flat-leaf parsley, chopped
1	onion, diced
3	fresh garlic cloves, diced
4	stalks celery, finely diced
8	plum tomatoes, peeled and diced
½	teaspoon oregano
1	teaspoon salt
1	teaspoon coarsely ground black pepper
1	teaspoon crushed red pepper, Optional
4	potatoes, peeled, cut into cubes
½	teaspoon sage
6	cups water
2	pounds fish, (halibut, snapper, tuna, swordfish)

In a large pot, add olive oil and heat. Add garlic, onion, celery and saute until tender. Add the potatoes, tomatoes, parsley, oregano, salt and pepper. Stir well and cook for 10 minutes over medium heat. Add water. Bring to a boil, then reduce heat to a simmer and cover. Continue to cook while stirring occasionally, until potatoes are tender, but not quite cooked. Depending on type of fish used, cut into 1 or 2 inch pieces or cubes. Add the fish to the pot, cover and simmer 15 minutes or until fish is tender.

Nutrition (per serving): 455 calories

Saturated Fat	1g
Total Fat	7g (14% of calories)
Protein	36g (32% of calories)
Carbohydrates	62g (55% of calories)
Cholesterol	65mg
Sodium	1020mg

My Notes and Recipe Variations

Soups, Side Dishes, and Other Tasty Stuff

French Onion Soup

Serves 10

Preparation :15   Cook :45   Stand :00   Total 1:00

Ingredients

6	large sweet onions, julienned (cut into strips)
1	stick butter
12	beef bouillon cubes
12	cups water
3	teaspoons Worcestershire sauce
1	teaspoon salt
½	teaspoon pepper
10	slices mozzarella cheese, (or use 2 cups shredded) or Swiss Cheese
10	slices French bread
2	teaspoons oil
1	fresh garlic clove, minced

Source: Merlo Bailey

In a large Dutch oven (4 to 6 quart), place butter and melt. Add onions and saute until tender. Add remaining ingredients, stirring well. Make sure that the bouillon cubes are broken up during the cooking process. Bring to a boil, then reduce heat to simmer. Cook for about 45 minutes, uncovered.

While soup is cooking, take French bread (about 2 inches in diameter) and cut 10 to 12 slices about 1 inch thick. Place oil and garlic in a small bowl and mix well. Let stand for 5-10 minutes. Preheat oven (or toaster oven) to 375 degrees. Place sliced bread on a baking sheet and lightly brush with oil and garlic mixture on both sides. Place on baking sheet. Bake for 8 minutes on 1 side, turn over and brush again, if needed. Bake for an additional 6-8 minutes, until bread is crunchy. Remove from oven and cool.

Place soup in broiler resistant bowls or small crocks. Place one large crouton (French bread slice) over soup, then place a slice of cheese on top (or sprinkle with grated mozzarella). Put under broiler until cheese slightly melts and is golden brown and bubbly. Remove from broiler and serve hot, being careful to not burn yourself or those enjoying this wonderful treat.

Nutrition (per serving): 171 calories

Saturated Fat	1g
Total Fat	3g (17% of calories)
Protein	5g (12% of calories)
Carbohydrates	30g (71% of calories)
Cholesterol	4mg
Sodium	1437mg

My Notes and Recipe Variations

Soups, Side Dishes, and Other Tasty Stuff

Minestrone Soup (Italian Vegetable Soup)

Serves 10

Preparation :10   Cook 1:30   Stand :00   Total 1:40

Serve this soup as a main meal or appetizer. Top with grated Romano cheese for flavor.

Ingredients

8	cups water
1	10 oz. package frozen chopped spinach
2	7-inch long zucchinis, chopped/diced
2	7-inch long yellow squash, chopped/diced
2	28 oz. cans canned stewed tomatoes
2	cups fresh green beans, cleaned and cut into 1-inch pieces
1	cup pasta, small, like tubetti, elbow macaroni, etc..., Optional
1	teaspoon salt
1	teaspoon black pepper
2	carrots, diced or sliced
1	10 oz. package frozen peas, Optional
½	cup frozen baby lima beans

frozen mixed vegetables, can be substituted for fresh vegetables (except tomatoes)

In a large pot with tight lid, add 2 tablespoons of olive oil. Heat. Add garlic, celery, parsley and saute till tender. Add water and stewed tomatoes. Bring water to a boil, then reduce to simmer. Add salt and pepper, cover and let simmer for 30-45 minutes.

Add carrots and continue to cook for an additional 5-7 minutes (depending on the type of pasta you are cooking) add pasta and cook for 5-7 minutes. When the pasta is done, add remaining vegetables to pot. Simmer for 5-7 minutes or until vegetables are tender, and spinach has thawed and soup is warm.

Nutrition (per serving): 94 calories

Saturated Fat	0g	
Total Fat	0g	(5% of calories)
Protein	4g	(18% of calories)
Carbohydrates	18g	(77% of calories)
Cholesterol	0mg	
Sodium	735mg	

My Notes and Recipe variations

Soups, Side Dishes, and Other Tasty Stuff

Minestrone Soup with Meat

Serves 10

Preparation :10   Cook 1:30   Stand :00   Total 1:40

Serve this soup as a main meal or appetizer. Top with grated romano cheese for flavor.

Ingredients

8	cups water
12	oz. frozen chopped spinach
3½	pounds canned stewed tomatoes
2	cups fresh green beans, cleaned and cut into 1-inch pieces
1	cup pasta, small, like tubetti, elbow macaroni, etc..., Optional
1	teaspoon salt
1	teaspoon black pepper
2	pounds chuck roast

In a pressure cooker or large pot with tight lid, add 2 tablespoons of olive oil. Heat. Add garlic, celery, parsley and saute until tender. Add boneless chuck roast. Lightly brown on one side. Turn roast over and brown. Add 2 cups of water. Bring water to a boil, then reduce to simmer. Add salt and pepper, cover and let simmer for 45 minutes to 1 hour.

If you are using a pressure cooker, add water to roast, cover and cook with 10# pressure. As soon as the pressure cooker begins to release steam, cook for 15-20 minutes or depending on the manufacturers recommendation.

Depending on the size of the roast used, more or less cooking may be necessary. Check midway to make sure there is enough liquid in the pan. (If using a pressure cooker, follow manufacturers directions for safe cooking). Remove cover and add stewed tomatoes and break using a wooden spoon. Add remaining water. Cover and simmer another 30-40 minutes, until meat begins breaking up. Bring the pot back to a boil and add the pasta. After 5-7 minutes, add remaining vegetables, stir and continue cooking until spinach thaws, pasta is cooked and soup is warm.

Remember:

Pressure cookers shorten cooking time. Make sure you follow manufacturers direction for safe cooking.

Nutrition (per serving): 326 calories

Saturated Fat	10g	
Total Fat	23g	(62% of calories)
Protein	18g	(22% of calories)
Carbohydrates	13g	(16% of calories)
Cholesterol	66mg	
Sodium	791mg	

My Notes and Recipe variations

Soups, Side Dishes, and Other Tasty Stuff

Mushroom and Onion Soup

Serves 4

Preparation :10   Cook :30   Stand :00   Total :40

This recipe, given to me by my friend and neighbor Merlo, is also great served over cheese Tortellini. This makes a great meal when served with crusty bread

Ingredients

1	cup fresh mushrooms, sliced
¼	cup butter
1½	cups onions, thinly sliced (or if you prefer diced)
2	cups beef broth, (or chicken broth) or 2 medium cans of broth
2½	cups water
½	teaspoon pepper
2	tablespoons dry white wine
2	teaspoons Worcestershire sauce (optional)
2	cups fresh cheese-filled tortellini

Source: Merlo Bailey

Using a saucepan (4 to 5 quart) melt the butter. Add mushrooms and onions and saute until tender. Add remaining ingredients and stir well. Cook over medium heat for 30 minutes. If you wish to add tortellini, add the tortellini about 10 minutes before soup is finished cooking. Sprinkle with Romano cheese and a little fresh parsley.

Nutrition (per serving): 280 calories

Saturated Fat	8g
Total Fat	15g (48% of calories)
Protein	9g (13% of calories)
Carbohydrates	26g (37% of calories)
Cholesterol	51mg
Sodium	672mg

My Notes and Recipe Variations

Soups, Side Dishes, and Other Tasty Stuff

Mushroom Barley Soup

Serves   6

Preparation   :15   Cook   1:30   Stand   :00   Total   1:45

Ingredients

1	sweet onion, chopped
3	stalks celery, diced
1 to 2	carrots, diced
1	pound fresh mushrooms, sliced
2	cups barley, rinsed well
2	tablespoons parsley, chopped
4	cups water
$4\frac{1}{2}$	cups vegetable broth or chicken broth (or three 12 oz. cans)
1	teaspoon basil
2	fresh garlic cloves, finely chopped
$\frac{1}{2}$	teaspoon salt
$\frac{1}{2}$	teaspoon white pepper

salt and pepper, to taste

In a large saucepan, add $\frac{1}{2}$ cup vegetable or chicken stock. Heat. Add celery, carrots, parsley, onion and garlic. Saute until tender. Add sliced mushrooms and continue to simmer, until mushrooms begin to soften. Add the remaining ingredients and bring to a boil. Reduce heat to low and simmer until the barley is tender and soup is thick (about 1 to $1\frac{1}{2}$ hours). Make sure that you stir occasionally so nothing sticks to the pan. Taste. Add salt and pepper to taste, if needed.

Nutrition (per serving): 408 calories

Saturated Fat	1g
Total Fat	3g (7% of calories)
Protein	12g (12% of calories)
Carbohydrates	82g (80% of calories)
Cholesterol	0mg
Sodium	2051mg

My Notes and Recipe Variations

Soups, Side Dishes, and Other Tasty Stuff

New England Clam Chowder

Serves 6-8

Preparation :15   Cook 1:20   Stand :00   Total 1:35

Ingredients

3	large onions, finely chopped
½	pound butter
20 to 30	large clams, cleaned and chopped (or 2 large cans of clams)
1	bottled clam juice, (only use if using fresh clams)
3	pounds white potatoes, peeled and cut into bite sized pieces
½	gallon milk, (whole milk adds a richer flavor, you can use reduced fat)
2 to 3	cups celery, finely chopped or sliced

In a large Dutch oven (or similar pan with cover, about 6-8 quart size), add butter and melt. Add onions and celery and saute until glossy and tender. Add cut up potatoes and saute for another 5-10 minutes. Add the clams and just enough clam juice to cover potatoes (if need be, add a little water).

If using canned clams, add clams (broth and all). Add a little water if need be. However, there should be enough juice to cover potatoes.

Cook over a low heat until potatoes are tender. Remove about ½ of potatoes and place on side. Add 1 gallon of milk, white pepper and salt to taste. Let cook until potatoes become over cooked and almost mushy (another 10 minutes or so). Mix well to break up potatoes; broth should begin to get a little thick. Add remaining potatoes, stir and cook for another 5-10 minutes. Serve hot.

Nutrition (per serving): 423 calories

Saturated Fat	31g
Total Fat	51g (50% of calories)
Protein	26g (11% of calories)
Carbohydrates	90g (39% of calories)
Cholesterol	166mg
Sodium	633mg

My Notes and Recipe Variations

Soups, Side Dishes, and Other Tasty Stuff

Pasta and Bean Soup (Zupa Pasta e Fagiuolo)

Serves 10

Preparation :10 Cook 4:00 Stand :00 Total 4:10

This is a fat free, hearty meal in a bowl. This bean soup is great to serve as an appetizer or as a hearty meal with garlic bread. Although the standard recipe calls for white beans, you can make it using the various 3-15 bean mixtures on the market.

Ingredients

4	stalks celery, diced
1	small onion, diced
2	tablespoons extra light olive oil
3	fresh garlic cloves, minced
$\frac{1}{2}$	teaspoon salt
$\frac{1}{2}$	teaspoon black pepper
1	12 oz. canned tomato sauce, (or one 28 oz. of canned tomatoes, cut up)
6	12 oz. cans water, (6 cups), more may need to be added later
1	cup white beans, dry
1	cup tiny soup pasta, dry

In a large pan, add olive oil, onion, celery, garlic, salt and pepper. Saute until tender. Add tomato sauce and 4 to 6 cans of water (using the tomato sauce can). Rinse beans in a colander under cool running water to remove any sediment. Add beans to soup mixture. Bring to a boil, then reduce heat and simmer for several hours, until beans are tender (4-6 hours). Stir occasionally to make sure nothing sticks to the bottom. As the soup cooks, the water will evaporate and the beans will also soak up the water as they swell and soften to double in size. (You may need to add a little more water before adding the pasta). Prior to adding pasta, make sure that there is enough liquid in the pot to cook the pasta. You may need to add a little more water. Add pasta and simmer for about 20-30 minutes, until pasta is al dente (tender, but firm). To speed the cooking process, you may wish to use 2 cans of white beans instead of the dry. Cook the soup for 2 hours, add pasta and when pasta is done (add the white beans, liquid and all). Heat for 10 minutes until beans are hot.

Variation:

You may wish to add 2 or 3 diced fresh carrots at the same time the pasta is added. The carrots will be done at the same time.

Nutrition (per serving): 171 calories

Saturated Fat	1g
Total Fat	4g (19% of calories)
Protein	6g (14% of calories)
Carbohydrates	29g (67% of calories)
Cholesterol	0mg
Sodium	683mg

My Notes and Recipe Variations

Soups, Side Dishes, and Other Tasty Stuff

Potato Soup

Serves   6

Preparation   :20   Cook   :45   Stand   :00   Total   1:05

Ingredients

1	quart chicken stock, (or use two 15 oz cans of chicken broth and two cans water)
4	cups potatoes, chopped or cut into bite sized pieces
2	cups carrots, sliced
1/2	teaspoon dill weed
2	tablespoons flour
1/2	cup celery, diced
1/4	cup onions, chopped
1	teaspoon salt
1/2	teaspoon white pepper
1	cup milk, (or half and half)

Source: Merlo Bailey

In a large Dutch oven, add chicken stock, potatoes, carrots, dill weed, celery, onion, salt and pepper. Mix well. Bring to a rolling boil and cook for 30 minutes. In a small covered jar, add milk and flour. Shake until smooth. Slowly pour the milk mixture into the soup, stirring constantly. Bring back to a boil. Remove from heat and cover.

For added flavor, you may wish to sprinkle with chives or Romano cheese when serving.

Nutrition (per serving): 202 calories

Saturated Fat	1g
Total Fat	2g (11% of calories)
Protein	6g (12% of calories)
Carbohydrates	39g (77% of calories)
Cholesterol	6mg
Sodium	1414mg

My Notes and Recipe variations

Soups, Side Dishes, and Other Tasty Stuff

vegetable Soup

Serves 6

Preparation :15 Cook :45 Stand :00 Total 1:00

Ingredients

2	quarts chicken stock, (or beef broth), about 8 cups
2	tablespoons extra light olive oil
2	fresh garlic cloves, chopped
1	medium sweet onion, chopped
2	cups white potatoes, cleaned (with skins), chopped into bite sized pieces
1	cup carrots, chopped into bite size pieces
1	cup broccoli florets
1	cup fresh green beans, (or use frozen)
1	cup cooked small white beans, Optional
1	parsnip, chopped into bite sized pieces

In a 4 to 6 quart Dutch oven (or pot with a cover), place oil and heat. Saute onions and garlic until tender. Add potatoes and parsnip and saute for 5-7 minutes, stirring so as not to burn.

Place chicken stock (if you wish you can use 4 cans of chicken broth with 4 cans of water). in pot and bring to a boil. Reduce heat to a simmer and cook until potatoes are almost cooked, slightly undercooked, about 20-30 minutes, depending on the size of the piece). Add remaining vegetables and simmer an additional 5-7 minutes. Add beans. Simmer for 5 minutes. Remove from heat.

Nutrition (per serving): 171 calories

Saturated Fat	1g	
Total Fat	6g	(33% of calories)
Protein	5g	(11% of calories)
Carbohydrates	24g	(56% of calories)
Cholesterol	0mg	
Sodium	2020mg	

My Notes and Recipe Variations

Soups, Side Dishes, and Other Tasty Stuff

Tortellini Soup

Serves 4

Preparation :05   Cook :25   Stand :00   Total :30

Ingredients

2	cups chicken broth
2	cups water
2	teaspoons fresh parsley, chopped
½	teaspoon pepper
2	tablespoons
1	pound tortellini, cheese or meat
¼	cup miso

Although using canned chicken stock is a quick and easy way to make this recipe, to get a full bodied flavor, you should use fresh chicken soup. Please reference the recipe for chicken soup in this section. When the soup is fully cooked, you may add the remaining ingredients to finalize the tortellini soup.

You may wish to make the fresh chicken soup. If in a hurry, the above recipe fits the bill for a quick and delicious meal. In a saucepan, add chicken broth, miso, water and pepper. Bring to a boil. Add parsley and tortellini. Cook until tender (15-20 minutes).

Nutrition (per serving): 406 calories

Saturated Fat	3g	
Total Fat	10g	(21% of calories)
Protein	20g	(20% of calories)
Carbohydrates	59g	(59% of calories)
Cholesterol	54mg	
Sodium	1775mg	

My Notes and Recipe Variations

Whiting Fish Soup

Serves 4

Preparation :10 Cook :30 Stand :00 Total :40

Ingredients

4	firm white fish
3	tablespoons extra light olive oil
½	cup unbleached flour
5	cloves fresh garlic cloves, finely chopped
1	teaspoon dried parsley

Source: Aunt Jean

Roll fish in flour. In large pot, add olive oil and garlic and heat. Add fish and lightly brown on all sides. Add 2-3 cups of water. Enough to fully cover the fish. Add salt and pepper to taste and parsley. Cover pot and cook over low to medium heat until fish is fully cooked (about 20 minutes).

In large soup bowl, place a piece of toasted hard Italian bread, or unseasoned large croutons. Place a fish and soup over bread. With any fish, please be careful of bones.

Nutrition (per serving): 332 calories

Saturated Fat	2g	
Total Fat	12g	(32% of calories)
Protein	43g	(52% of calories)
Carbohydrates	13g	(16% of calories)
Cholesterol	99mg	
Sodium	126mg	

My Notes and Recipe Variations

Zucchini Bisque

Serves 6

Preparation :15 Cook :30 Stand :00 Total :45

You can also substitute the zucchini for shrimp and add 1 to 2 teaspoons paprika for a great Shrimp Bisque.

Ingredients

2	tablespoons butter
2	cups zucchini, cleaned and sliced
1	cup fresh mushrooms, sliced
½	cup onions, chopped
¼	cup fresh parsley, chopped
3	tablespoons butter
3	tablespoons unbleached flour
1	10 oz. can chicken broth, (or 1¼ cup homemade chicken broth)
1	cup whipping cream
¼	teaspoon white pepper

Source: Merlo Bailey

In a 4 to 6 quart saucepan, add 2 tablespoons butter and melt. Add zucchini, mushrooms, onions and parsley. Saute until tender. Remove from pan. Add 3 tablespoons butter and stir in flour using a fork or wire whisk until smooth. Add chicken broth and mix well. Continue cooking on low to medium until soup is thickened. Stir in cream and pepper. Add zucchini mixture, stir well, heat to serving temperature and serve.

Variation:

If using shrimp (about 10-15 medium sized shrimp, cut into bite sized pieces) saute as recommended for zucchini. Remove from pan and place in soup at end. Add paprika to chicken broth mixture.

Nutrition (per serving): 263 calories

Saturated Fat	15g	
Total Fat	25g	(85% of calories)
Protein	3g	(4% of calories)
Carbohydrates	8g	(12% of calories)
Cholesterol	80mg	
Sodium	403mg	

My Notes and Recipe Variations

Soups, Side Dishes, and Other Tasty Stuff

Thick Crust Pizza

Serves   6

Preparation   :30   Cook   1:30   Stand   :00   Total   2:00

Can't find a good pizza anywhere? This recipe will make one very thick crust pizza and you can control the amount of toppings (see suggestions below). Try making one at home.

Ingredients

3	cups unbleached flour
1	cup warm water, about 120 degrees
1	package active dry yeast
1	teaspoon salt
1	pound mozzarella cheese, shredded
1	28 oz. can crushed tomato, drained well
2	teaspoons ready-to-use garlic, diced (or 1 teaspoon garlic powder)
1	teaspoon dried oregano
1	tablespoon sesame seeds
2	tablespoons olive oil, plus extra for brushing crust
$\frac{1}{4}$	teaspoon dried basil
2	tablespoons corn meal
1	tablespoon sesame seeds
2	tablespoons olive oil, plus extra for brushing crust

In a large bowl add flour, yeast, 1 teaspoon salt and 1½ cups of the flour. By hand, or using a mixer at low speed, add very warm water. Mix well. At a medium speed, begin adding remaining flour. When dough becomes too thick to use with the mixer, use your hands to further blend to a soft dough. Remove dough from bowl and place on a lightly floured surface. Knead dough for at least 10 minutes. Place in lightly greased bowl and cover with towel Allow to rise until doubled (about 2 ½ hours).

When dough is raised, punch down and knead another 5 minutes. Roll dough to fit a deep dish pizza pan. Generously oil the pan and add the dough, making sure that you bring dough up the sides. Take well drained crushed tomatoes and put in a bowl. Add the fresh diced garlic (if using garlic powder, omit this step). Let sit for 20 minutes. After sitting, take tomato mixture and cover bottom of dough. Spread the tomatoes evenly. If you have an extra large pan you will probably need another can of tomatoes. If using garlic powder, sprinkle tomatoes with garlic powder and oregano. If you are using sausage or other toppings. Add a little more garlic powder and oregano. Bake in a 425 degree oven for 20 minutes to reduce moisture. Remove and place mozzarella evenly over toppings. Return to oven, reducing to 375 degrees and bake an additional 10-15 minutes, until mozzarella is melted and golden brown.

If you are only making a cheese pizza. Bake in preheated 350-375 degree oven for approximately 25 minutes, until cheese is melted and golden.

Toppings:

1. Sausage—(remove sausage from casing—about 3 or 4 links) and saute in skillet until done. Drain and blot well with paper towels.

2. Green pepper—clean and cut into eighths. Steam until tender or use raw for a crunchier pizza.

3. Instead of tomato sauce, use fresh plum or Italian tomatoes. Cut into slice and saute in skillet with a little olive oil until liquid evaporates. Make sure you sprinkle with garlic powder and oregano for full Italian flavor.

4. Raw onion—cut onion into slices, strips or diced, place on pizza. To remove excess water, gently saute without oil.

5. Broccoli florets—(small pieces), blanched.

6. Mushrooms—(raw and sliced)

7. Pepperoni—thinly sliced

8. Anchovy fillets—well drained and blotted with paper towel. Sometimes I add chopped anchovy to the sauce while simmering for a less overpowering taste).

9. Black olives—sliced.

Nutrition (per serving): 617 calories

Saturated Fat	12g	
Total Fat	28g	(41% of calories)
Protein	25g	(16% of calories)
Carbohydrates	66g	(43% of calories)
Cholesterol	59mg	
Sodium	704mg	

My Notes and Recipe Variations

Thin Crust Pizza

Preparation :20   Cook :45   Stand :00   Total 1:05

Can't find a good pizza anywhere? This recipe will make one very thick crust pizza and you can control the amount of toppings (see suggestions below). Try making one at home.

Ingredients

3	cups unbleached flour
1	cup warm water, about 120 degrees
1	package active dry yeast
1	teaspoon salt
1	pound mozzarella cheese, shredded
1	16 oz. can crushed tomato
1	6 oz. can tomato paste
2	fresh garlic cloves, diced
1	small sweet onion, diced, Optional
1	teaspoon dried oregano
1/4	teaspoon dried basil
2	tablespoons corn meal
1	tablespoon sesame seeds
2	tablespoons olive oil, plus extra for brushing crust

In a large bowl add flour, yeast, 1 teaspoon salt and 1½ cups of the flour. By hand, or using a mixer at low speed, add very warm water. Mix well. At a medium speed, begin adding remaining flour. When dough becomes too thick to use with the mixer, use your hands to further blend to a soft dough. Remove dough from bowl and place on a lightly floured surface. Knead dough for at least 10 minutes. Place in lightly greased bowl and cover with towel. Allow to rise until doubled (about 2 ½ hours).

In saucepan, add 2 tablespoons olive oil, garlic, and spices. Saute until garlic is tender. Add tomatoes and break with wooden spoon. Add tomato paste and stir well until paste is fully blended. Simmer for 30 minutes. When dough has risen, punch down and knead another 5 minutes. Separate dough into 2 pieces. Roll each piece out to fit on pizza pan. If you desire a slightly thicker crust, use more dough (or add 1 cup flour and ⅓ cup warm water to original recipe). Oil pizza pan. Take 1 tablespoon of corn meal and spread on bottom of pan. Lay dough on pan. Spread with sauce. Sprinkle with ½ the mozzarella cheese.

Bake in 375 degree oven for approximately 20 minutes, until cheese is melted and golden.

Toppings:

1. Sausage—(remove sausage from casing and saute in skillet until done. Drain and blot well with paper towels

2. Green pepper—clean and cut into eighths. Steam until tender or use raw for a crunchier pizza

3. Instead of tomato sauce, use fresh plum or Italian tomatoes. Cut into slices and saute in skillet with a little olive oil until liquid evaporates. Make sure you sprinkle with garlic powder and oregano for full Italian flavor.

4. Raw onion—cut onion into slices, strips or diced, place on pizza. To remove excess water, gently saute without oil.

5. Broccoli florets—(small pieces), blanched.

6. Mushrooms—(raw and sliced).

7. Pepperoni—thinly sliced.

8. Anchovy fillets—well drained and blotted with paper towel. Sometimes I add chopped anchovy to the sauce while simmering for a less overpowering taste).

9. Black olives—sliced.

Nutrition (per serving): 849 calories

Saturated Fat	16g	
Total Fat	34g	(36% of calories)
Protein	37g	(17% of calories)
Carbohydrates	98g	(46% of calories)
Cholesterol	89mg	
Sodium	1065mg	

My Notes and Recipe Variations

Soups, Side Dishes, and Other Tasty Stuff

Pizza Fritta (Fried Bread)

Serves   4

Preparation   :20   Cook   :10   Stand   :00   Total   :30

This recipe can be made as a dessert or as a snack similar to a small pizza

Ingredients

2	cups unbleached flour, sifted
2	teaspoons baking powder
1	teaspoon salt
1	large egg
3	tablespoons Cannola oil
½	cup water

In a mixing bowl, sift flour, baking powder and salt. Beat egg in a small bowl and stir in oil and water. Pour over dry ingredients and mix well with a fork. Turn out dough onto a lightly floured surface and knead until smooth. Divide the dough in half. Take one piece and flatten out on a lightly oiled surface (to fit in medium skillet). Heat some cooking oil in a skillet until hot. Fry the rolled out dough in the pan, on both sides until light golden and puffy. Remove from pan and place on paper towel to drain excess oil. Fry remaining dough.

Serving suggestion:
Sprinkle with sugar or for an after school snack, spread pizza sauce and a little mozzarella cheese.

Nutrition (per serving): 334 calories

Saturated Fat	1g	
Total Fat	12g	(33% of calories)
Protein	8g	(10% of calories)
Carbohydrates	48g	(58% of calories)
Cholesterol	53mg	
Sodium	780mg	

My Notes and Recipe Variations

Calzone

Serves 20

Prep 2:30 Cook 1:00 Stand :00 Total 3:30

Ingredients

1	cube yeast
1	cup warm water
4	cups unbleached flour
1	teaspoon salt
2	teaspoons extra light olive oil
2	pounds Italian sausage
2	pounds ricotta cheese
½	cup Romano cheese, grated
½	cup parsley, minced
6	eggs
1	teaspoon salt
1	teaspoon black pepper

Source: Grandma Maria Zappavigna

Dough:

Dissolve yeast in 1 cup of lukewarm water. In a large bowl, add 4 cup flour and make a hole or well in the middle of the flour and add salt and yeast mixture. Knead dough for about 10 minutes. Add oil and continue kneading until smooth. (You may also place dough on lightly floured surface and continue kneading until smooth). When dough is fully kneaded, place in bowl, cover with wax paper and towel and set in warm place and let rise for 2 hours. Begin making filling.

Filling:

Cut sausage in ½ inch pieces. In large skillet, fry sausage until brown. Drain well and place sausage on paper towel to remove excess oil. In a large bowl, cream ricotta cheese and add eggs, one at a time, blending well. Add Romano cheese, parsley, salt and pepper, while mixing well. Add fried sausage to cheese mixture. Place in refrigerator until dough has fully raised.

When dough has raised for 2 hours, grease a 15x11x2 inch pan with salad oil. Remove dough from bowl, 'punch' down and knead for several more minutes. Roll down out to fit into pan, ensuring that about 1 to 1½ inch of dough is brought up around the sides of the pan. When dough is placed fully in pan, spread the filling mixture evenly over bottom.

Bake in a 350 degree oven for 45 minutes to 1 hour (or until knife inserted in the center of filling comes out clean).

Nutrition (per serving): 360 calories

Saturated Fat	10g	
Total Fat	23g	(57% of calories)
Protein	17g	(19% of calories)
Carbohydrates	22g	(24% of calories)
Cholesterol	123mg	
Sodium	651mg	

My Notes and Recipe Variations

Halupke (Slavic Style Stuffed Cabbage)

Serves 10

Preparation :20 Cook 2:00 Stand :00 Total 2:20

Ingredients

1	small head cabbage
½	cup raw rice
1½	pounds boneless pork shoulder, ground
1	egg
1	teaspoon salt
½	teaspoon pepper
1 to 1½	pounds sauerkraut
1	8 oz. tomato sauce
1 to 2	cups sour cream

Core cabbage and cook in boiling water for a few minutes to softened leaves so they can easily be separated from head. In a separate bowl, add ground pork, rice, egg, salt and pepper and mix well. Cut the heaviest part of membrane from each cabbage leaf. Place a large spoonful of filling in each cabbage leaf, fold over the sides, and roll up the cabbage. Tie with a string to secure. Place the filled cabbage (Halupke) in the bottom of a Dutch oven and layer until all cabbage and filling are used. Cover with sauerkraut (including juice). Mix 1 cup of sour cream with tomato sauce and pour mixture over top of sauerkraut. Cover pot and cook over a low heat for 1½ to 2 hours. Serve topped with a dollop of sour cream.

Variation:
If you don't care for sauerkraut you can still make this recipe and omit sauerkraut.

Nutrition (per serving): 231 calories

Saturated Fat	4g	
Total Fat	11g	(43% of calories)
Protein	17g	(29% of calories)
Carbohydrates	16g	(28% of calories)
Cholesterol	76mg	
Sodium	752mg	

My Notes and Recipe Variations

Soups, Side Dishes, and Other Tasty Stuff

Glumky-Stuffed Cabbage (Pigs in a Blanket)

Serves   6

Preparation   :10   Cook   2:00   Stand   :00   Total   2:10

Ingredients

2	pounds lean ground beef
1½	cups rice
1	egg
1	teaspoon salt
1	teaspoon pepper
1	tablespoon dried parsley
1	28 oz. can crushed tomato
1	12 oz. tomato sauce
2	cups water
1	teaspoon salt
1	teaspoon black pepper
1	head green cabbage

Fill a large pot with 6 quarts of water and 1 tablespoon salt. Place whole cabbage into boiling water and boil briskly, uncovered, for 10 minutes. Remove cabbage and carefully detach as many of the softened leaves as possible. Return what is left of the whole cabbage to the boiling water and cook a little longer to allow you to detach more leaves.

In the same pot of water, add crushed tomato and tomato sauce. Add a little more water, if need be. Add salt and pepper to taste. Bring to a boil. In a mixing bowl, add ground beef, rice, 1 teaspoon salt, 1 teaspoon pepper and dried parsley, mix well. Take a leaf of cabbage and add meat mixture (about the size of 2 or 3 golf balls), shape into a rectangle and place in center of cabbage. Fold over thickest end, next fold in the sides and roll until end of cabbage piece. Using string or thread tie the stuffed cabbage crosswise and lengthwise. Place on side and continue making until all meat is used. When all glumky are made, reduce heat on tomato sauce to simmer and add the glumky to the sauce. Cook for 30-45 minutes, until done. Remove glumky from sauce and add cut up potatoes. Cook until tender. Return glumky to sauce to heat. Place in a large serving bowl.

Nutrition (per serving): 699 calories

Saturated Fat	13g	
Total Fat	33g	(42% of calories)
Protein	36g	(21% of calories)
Carbohydrates	65g	(37% of calories)
Cholesterol	149mg	
Sodium	1296mg	

My Notes and Recipe Variations

Soups, Side Dishes, and Other Tasty Stuff

Stuffed Peppers

Serves   4

Preparation   :15   Cook   1:20   Stand   :00   Total   1:35

Stuffed peppers and stuffed cabbage were a favorite in our house, easy and economical to make. You can also make the stuffed peppers without meat.

Ingredients

1	pound lean ground beef
1	cup raw rice, instant is fine
1	28 oz. can crushed tomato
1	teaspoon salt
1	teaspoon black pepper
1	egg
2	fresh garlic cloves, minced
1	teaspoon oregano, or sage, basil, depending on flavor you desire
4	large green bell peppers
1	12 oz. tomato sauce
2	cups water

Clean green peppers, by cutting out core and removing seeds and wash. In a mixing bowl, add ground beef, salt, pepper, egg and rice. Mix well. Divide meat mixture into fourths and stuff the green pepper with the meat mixture. In a large pot, add 2 tablespoons oil and heat. Put filled green peppers, stuffed side down, on pan and saute for 3 minutes. This will sear the meat and keep it in the pepper. Turn pepper and stand on its end. Add 1 can crushed tomato, 1 can tomato sauce and water. Stir well. Make sure green peppers are covered with sauce. Add garlic, oregano, salt and pepper to taste. Bring to a boil, then reduce to a simmer. Cover pot and cook for 45 minutes to 1 hour (until meat is cooked). Rice will swell and absorb some of the liquid. Remove stuffed peppers from sauce and add 4 cut up potatoes and cook until tender. Serve green peppers with boiled potatoes. Place some of the sauce in a gravy boat and serve for the potatoes. Some people like to make extra meat without the green peppers. Simply increase the meat and rice in equal amounts.

Vegetarian Stuffed Peppers:

3-4 cups of mixed vegetables (these can be leftover vegetables mixed together). 1 cup of cooked rice or 1 cup of bread crumbs, salt pepper, garlic as above. Mix all of the ingredients together. Cut green peppers in half and fill the pepper with the vegetable mixture. Place in a baking dish. Place ½ of the crushed tomatoes in the bottom of the baking dish and add ½ cup water. Stir. Place peppers (vegetable side up) in the tomatoes. Add remaining crushed tomatoes to the top of each stuffed pepper. Bake in a 350 degree oven for approximately 20 minutes (until vegetable mixture is hot and green pepper is tender). Serve hot.

Nutrition (per serving): 641 calories

Saturated Fat	10g
Total Fat	26g (36% of calories)
Protein	30g (19% of calories)
Carbohydrates	72g (45% of calories)
Cholesterol	138mg
Sodium	1239mg

My Notes and Recipe Variations

Soups, Side Dishes, and Other Tasty Stuff

Wild Rice Dressing or Stuffing

Serves   6

Preparation :30 Cook 1:00 Stand :15 Total 1:45

Use as a side dish or to stuff a Cornish Game Hen.

Ingredients

½	cup long grain wild rice
½	cup brown rice
1	tablespoon extra virgin olive oil
2	cups fresh mushrooms, sliced/diced
1	cup celery, chopped
1	large yellow onion, chopped
½	cup chicken broth
½	cup water
½	teaspoon salt
½	teaspoon black pepper
2	fresh garlic cloves, chopped

Cook wild rice and brown rice (in separate pots) as package directs. In a large skillet (preferably cast iron), spray with non-stick oil. Over medium heat, saute onions, garlic, celery and mushrooms until tender. Add to rice mixture, mixing well Add the chicken broth and water. Put into a Dutch oven and bake in a 350 degree oven for 30 minutes, uncovered. Stir dressing and cover. Cook for an additional 30 minutes. (This can also be used as a stuffing with turkey or chicken). Stuff turkey or chicken and truss it. Then insert thermometer in thigh. Roast turkey or chicken on a rack for 30 minutes at 425 degrees. Lower temperature to 375 degree (or 350 degrees depending on your oven) and cook the remainder of the time until the thermometer registers done.

Nutrition (per serving): 129 calories

Saturated Fat	1g	
Total Fat	3g	(24% of calories)
Protein	3g	(9% of calories)
Carbohydrates	21g	(67% of calories)
Cholesterol	0mg	
Sodium	405mg	

My Notes and Recipe variations

Soups, Side Dishes, and Other Tasty Stuff

Mushroom and Onion Crouton Dressing-Stuffing

Serves   6

Preparation :30   Cook 1:00   Stand :15   Total 1:45

Looking for different ways to enhance turkey, chicken or pork recipes. Try this mouth-watering dressing.

Ingredients

1	cup celery, diced, Optional
1	cup medium sweet onion, diced
1	cup fresh mushrooms, sliced
4	cups croutons
1/4	cup fresh parsley, chopped
1/2	teaspoon salt
1/2	teaspoon coarsely ground black pepper
2	fresh garlic cloves, minced
1	cup chicken broth

In a large heated skillet, add butter and melt. Add salt, pepper, celery, onion, mushrooms, parsley and garlic. Saute until tender. Add broth and mix well. In a Dutch oven (or other oven proof container, add croutons). To the croutons add the vegetable mixture and mix well. Cook in a 350 degree oven for 1 hour. This can also be used to stuff a turkey or chicken.

Nutrition (per serving): 181 calories

Saturated Fat	2g	
Total Fat	7g	(37% of calories)
Protein	6g	(13% of calories)
Carbohydrates	23g	(50% of calories)
Cholesterol	0mg	
Sodium	811mg	

My Notes and Recipe Variations

Barbecue Sauce and Marinade for Spare Ribs

Serves   1

Preparation :05   Cook :00   Stand :00   Total :05

Ingredients

1	cup catsup
1/3	cup Worcestershire sauce
1	teaspoon chili powder
1	teaspoon salt
1/4	teaspoon Tabasco sauce, (more if you like more bite)
1	cup water
2	fresh garlic cloves, minced
1/2	cup dry red wine, (or wine vinegar)

Source: Merlo Bailey

Mix all ingredients in a small bowl. Let stand for 15 to 30 minutes so flavors can enhance the sauce. Place ribs in a air-tight container and cover with sauce. Let marinade for at least 1 hour (or overnight). Place ribs on grill or in broiler and cook.

Continue to baste with marinade for added flavor and to ensure the ribs do not dry out.

Nutrition: 311 calories

Saturated Fat	0g
Total Fat	1g (4% of calories)
Protein	5g (6% of calories)
Carbohydrates	71g (91% of calories)
Cholesterol	0mg
Sodium	5401mg

My Notes and Recipe variations

Oyster Dressing

Serves   8

Preparation   :30   Cook   3:00   Stand   :15   Total   3:45

This recipe is easy to make for either chicken or turkey meals and is great for Thanksgiving or anytime. Please read the 'Suggestion' section for calorie and fat reductions and cooking time reduction.

Ingredients

10	stalks large celery stalks, cleaned, cut, diced
½	stick margarine or butter
1	package giblets
2	loaves white bread, day old or stuffing bread
1	8 oz. oysters with liquid, cut, Optional
1	16 oz. can chicken broth, Optional
1	cup water, Optional

In a large pan, add diced celery pieces. Fill pot with water to 1 inch above celery. Add margarine or butter. Cook over medium heat until tender.

In a smaller pot, add giblets and turkey or chicken neck. Cover with water and cook until done; about 30 minutes. In a large roasting pan, break up the bread into pieces. (The bread, celery and giblets can be done the night before to save time on Thanksgiving day. Don't worry if the bread gets hard, it will soften when you make the dressing).

To the bread in the large roasting pan add the cooked celery, water, broth from the giblets and chopped giblets. Also add the oysters and their liquid. (If you are gun shy about touching raw oysters, poach them in hot water for a few minutes, until cooked, then cut them up and add to bread mixture). Mix all ingredients thoroughly and place roasting pan in a 350 degree oven for 3-5 hours. Approximately every 30 minutes check the dressing and stir. The dressing will begin to thicken as the liquid is absorbed and evaporates. Sides will get crusty.

NOTE:

If you are cooking a turkey, you may wish to add some of the turkey drippings (or juices) every hour or so to the dressing for more flavor and moisture. If you do not wish to use the turkey or chicken drippings, or are cooking turkey or chicken breasts, you can use 1 to 2 cans of chicken broth and 1 to 2 cups of water, mixed into the dressing.

Nutrition (per serving): 51 calories

Saturated Fat	0g	
Total Fat	2g	(26% of calories)
Protein	3g	(23% of calories)
Carbohydrates	7g	(51% of calories)
Cholesterol	25mg	
Sodium	117mg	

My Notes and Recipe Variations

Soups, Side Dishes, and Other Tasty Stuff

Auntie Dolores' Spaghetti Sauce

Serves Approx 30 1/2 cup servings

Preparation :10 Cook 2:30 Stand :00 Total 2:40

Aunt Dolores' spaghetti sauce was always a favorite of mine and I use to enjoy this sauce for a great change of pace.

Ingredients

1 to 2	pounds ribs, ranch style, Optional
2	pounds ground round
2	tablespoons salt
2	teaspoons allspice
1	teaspoon sage
2	carrots
7 to 8	celery, ribs/stalks
2	tablespoons parsley flakes
2	28 oz. cans tomato puree
1	28 oz. can water
2	16 oz. cans tomato paste
1	16 oz. can water
2	6 oz. cans tomato paste
1	6 oz. can water
1	stick butter, or margarine
2	pounds ground pork
2	teaspoons basil
$\frac{1}{2}$	teaspoon cinnamon
6	fresh garlic cloves
2	medium sweet onion
pepper, to taste	

Source: Gloria Kuska

Using a large Dutch oven (or pot) with cover, brown ground pork and ground round meat and drain the fat. Add spices to the meat, reduce to a low or medium heat. While meat in cooking, chop all vegetables in a food processor (or by hand). Add vegetables to meat and cook for 15 minutes. Add tomato puree, tomato sauce and tomato paste, mix well. Add ribs, water, mix and cook for at least $2\frac{1}{2}$ hours. The longer the sauce cooks the more flavorful and thick it becomes. Remove from heat and add the butter. Stir until melted. Cool. Serve over spaghetti. You can also place in containers and freeze for use at a future date.

Nutrition (per serving): 7784 calories

Saturated fat	132g	
Total Fat	341g	(39% of calories)
Protein	482g	(25% of calories)
Carbohydrates	697g	(36% of calories)
Cholesterol	1373mg	
Sodium	22124mg	

My Notes and Recipe variations

Beef Marinade

Serves   1

Preparation   :10   Cook   :00   Stand   3:00   Total   3:10

Excellent marinade for London Broil.

Ingredients

¼	cup oil
½	teaspoon garlic powder, (or 1 teaspoon fresh minced garlic)
2	tablespoons lemon juice, fresh
2	teaspoons soy sauce
2	tablespoons green onions, chopped
1	teaspoon coarsely ground black pepper
1	teaspoon celery salt

Mix all ingredients. Place in an airtight container and add meat. Marinade at least 2 hours (overnight is best). Reserve marinade for basting meat during broiling or grilling. Retain leftover marinade and pour over meat when it is done cooking.

Nutrition (per serving): 536 calories

Saturated Fat	3g
Total Fat	55g (92% of calories)
Protein	2g (1% of calories)
Carbohydrates	9g (7% of calories)
Cholesterol	0mg
Sodium	2247mg

My Notes and Recipe Variations

Basil Pesto

Preparation :10 Cook :00 Stand :00 Total :10

Ingredients

3	tablespoons Pignoli, (pine nuts)
3	fresh garlic cloves
¼	cup Pecorino Romano cheese
¼	teaspoon crushed red pepper
1	cup extra virgin olive oil
½	cup Italian flat-leaf parsley
60	fresh basil leaves, (60-100)

In a food processor, add parsley and basil leaves. Blend or chop. Add Pignoli (pine nuts), garlic and Romano cheese blended or chopped. While processor is rotating on high, SLOWLY add the olive oil until mixture is smooth. The mixture should be somewhat loose to allow even coating of pasta.

This recipe is also great served over Cheese Ravioli.

Nutrition (per serving): 368 calories

Nutritional information based upon serving 6

Saturated Fat	6g	
Total Fat	39g	(96% of calories)
Protein	2g	(2% of calories)
Carbohydrates	2g	(2% of calories)
Cholesterol	3mg	
Sodium	45mg	

My Notes and Recipe variations

_____

_____

_____

_____

_____

Cucumber Dressing

Serves   6

Preparation :10   Cook :00   Stand :15   Total :25

Ingredients

1	cup plain yogurt
½	cup sour cream, or mayonnaise
1 to 2	tablespoons white wine vinegar
½	cucumber, peeled, sliced and chopped
1	tablespoon lemon juice
2	teaspoons dill weed
2	teaspoons fresh parsley, chopped

salt and pepper, to taste

Blend all ingredients except cucumber and parsley together in a blender or by hand with a wire wisk and bowl. Mix until smooth. Fold in cucumber and parsley. Refridgerate for best flavor.

Nutrition (per serving): 71 calories

Saturated Fat	2g	
Total Fat	5g	(68% of calories)
Protein	2g	(12% of calories)
Carbohydrates	4g	(20% of calories)
Cholesterol	12mg	
Sodium	91mg	

My Notes and Recipe Variations

Creamy Italian Dressing

Serves 6

Preparation :10 Cook :00 Stand :10 Total :20

Ingredients

1/2	cup sour cream
1/2	cup mayonnaise, or sour cream
2	tablespoons lemon juice
2	tablespoons red wine vinegar
2	fresh garlic cloves, minced or crushed with a garlic press
1	teaspoon oregano
1	small onion, or scallion finely diced or minced
1	teaspoon crushed red pepper, sweet or mild (or one teaspoon bell pepper minced)
2	tablespoons extra light olive oil

salt and pepper, to taste

Blend all ingredients together until smooth and creamy. Place in a sealed container in the refridgerator to ensure all flavors blend. (If need be add a little more olive oil for a smoother consistency). Serve over greens

Nutrition (per serving): 226 calories

Saturated Fat	5g	
Total Fat	23g	(93% of calories)
Protein	1g	(1% of calories)
Carbohydrates	2g	(4% of calories)
Cholesterol	14mg	
Sodium	181mg	

My Notes and Recipe Variations

Creamy Italian Garlic Dressing

Serves 10

Preparation :10 Cook :00 Stand :15 Total :25

Ingredients

¾	cup light olive oil
¾	cup Cannola oil
3	fresh garlic cloves, crushed
2	teaspoons salt
1	teaspoon coarsely ground black pepper
½	cup tarragon wine vinegar
1	teaspoon oregano
1	teaspoon dry mustard
1	egg, Optional

In a blender, add Cannola oil and remaining ingredients. Blend on low speed for 2 minutes. While blending, slowly add olive oil until well blended. Refrigerate overnight before using. Serve over salad.

Variation:
You can also add 1 tablespoon of minced onion flakes.

Nutrition (per serving): 300 calories

Saturated Fat	3g	
Total Fat	33g	(98% of calories)
Protein	0g	(0% of calories)
Carbohydrates	1g	(2% of calories)
Cholesterol	0mg	
Sodium	470mg	

My Notes and Recipe Variations

Garlic Dressing

Serves 6

Preparation :05 Cook :00 Stand :00 Total :05

Ingredients

2	tablespoons lemon juice
1	cup mayonnaise
2 to 3	fresh garlic cloves, minced or crushed in a garlic press
1	tablespoon extra light olive oil
1	tablespoon wine vinegar

Place all ingredients in a blender (or use a wire whisk and bowl). Blend well. If you desire a slightly thinner dressing, add a little more oil until the right consistency. Pour over salad.

Nutrition (per serving): 290 calories

Saturated Fat	6g	
Total Fat	32g	(99% of calories)
Protein	0g	(0% of calories)
Carbohydrates	1g	(1% of calories)
Cholesterol	13mg	
Sodium	215mg	

My Notes and Recipe Variations

_____
_____
_____
_____
_____
_____
_____

Eggplant Sauce

Serves   6

Preparation   :10   Cook   :30   Stand   :00   Total   :40

This sauce is excellent served over pasta or with a meaty fish such as swordfish, halibut steaks or with crustaceans (shrimp, scallops).

Ingredients

1	large green bell pepper
1	small onion
1½	pounds eggplant
¼	cup extra virgin olive oil
1	16 oz. can tomato sauce
1	cup dry red wine
2	garlic cloves, minced
6	Italian tomatoes, peeled and cubed

salt and pepper, to taste

Clean the bell pepper and cut into bite sized pieces. Cut the ends off the eggplant and peel. Cube the eggplant into bite sized pieces. Cut and dice onion. Place the tomatoes into a pot of boiling water and let sit for 2-3 minutes. Remove from water and peel off the skin. Cube the tomatoes.

Using a large skillet (12 inches at least), add olive oil and heat. Add garlic, green pepper and onion. Saute until tender. Add tomato sauce, wine and cubed eggplant and tomatoes. Simmer for 20-25 minutes, until well blended and vegetables are tender. Serve over pasta.

Variation:

Add 14-18 small to medium shrimp at end. Serve over pasta.

Nutrition (per serving): 183 calories

Saturated Fat	1 g
Total Fat	10g (48% of calories)
Protein	4g (8% of calories)
Carbohydrates	20g (45% of calories)
Cholesterol	0mg
Sodium	540mg

My Notes and Recipe variations

Soups, Side Dishes, and Other Tasty Stuff

Four Cheese Sauce

Serves   4

Preparation   :05   Cook   :15   Stand   :00   Total   :20

This recipe makes enough for 8-10 oz of pasta, served as a side dish. Simply double recipe to serve more hearty appetites

Ingredients

1	cup whole milk
½	cup sour cream, (or ½ cup softened cream cheese)
2	teaspoons Italian flat-leaf parsley, chopped
2	teaspoons Romano cheese
2	teaspoons Parmesan cheese
1	teaspoon provolone cheese, sharp, grated (or blue cheese)
1	teaspoon ready-to-use garlic, minced, Optional

Except for Sour Cream, Put all ingredients in a blender and mix on pulsed/low for several minutes. In a saucepan, add cheese mixture and cook over medium heat until it starts to boil. Reduce heat to simmer and cook for 5 minutes (making sure all cheese is blended). Blend in the sour cream. Toss over 8-10 ounces of small pasta (such as rigatoni, penne, meza rigatoni, orecchiette.

This sauce will thicken as it cools. Serve immediately.

Variation:
Add during simmering process.
1. Take 2 cups of cooked chicken (leftover chicken breasts, thigh or leg meat) and add to sauce while simmering. Toss with pasta.
2. Add ½ pound cooked shrimp.
3. Add zucchini or yellow squash.

Nutrition (per serving): 112 calories

Saturated Fat	4g	
Total Fat	9g	(72% of calories)
Protein	4g	(13% of calories)
Carbohydrates	4g	(15% of calories)
Cholesterol	22mg	
Sodium	73mg	

My Notes and Recipe Variations

Soups, Side Dishes, and Other Tasty Stuff

Fra Diavolo (Spicy Spaghetti Sauce)

Serves   6

Preparation   :15   Cook   :30   Stand   :10   Total   :55

This sauce is great served over pasta, with or without shrimp and scallops, or over a bed of greens.

Ingredients

2	pounds Italian tomatoes (POMODORO), peeled and quartered (canned or fresh)
2	teaspoons extra virgin olive oil
1	Spanish onion, finely diced
2	fresh garlic cloves, diced
1/4	cup fresh parsley, chopped
1/4	cup dry red wine, Optional
2	teaspoons crushed red pepper, (or as much as you desire)
1	teaspoon salt
1/2	teaspoon black pepper
1/2	teaspoon oregano
1	teaspoon fresh basil leaves, finely chopped
1	pound spaghetti
1/2	cup extra virgin olive oil, (if serving over greens, otherwise omit)
1	tablespoon lemon juice
3/4	pound spinach, used instead of pasta, Optional
1/2	pound escarole, (or endive, used instead of pasta, Optional

Prepare all ingredients as follows:

Bring pot of water to a boil. Core tomato and make 2 light slits in bottom of tomato (like a cross). Add each tomato one at a time and leave for 20-30 seconds. Remove from water and peel skin off from the slits made. Peel and dice garlic cloves, Spanish onion and parsley. In a large skillet, add 2 tablespoons olive oil and heat. Add crushed red pepper, garlic and onion and cook until tender. Add lemon juice and wine (optional) and stir. Add tomatoes (quartered for plum tomatoes, in eights for regular tomatoes) including juice. Stir. Add parsley, basil, oregano, salt and pepper to taste. Stir to make sure all ingredients are thoroughly mixed. (cook on simmer for an additional 15-30 minutes). Serve over spaghetti.

If serving over greens, as an appetizer: Follow directions above except use only 1 clove of chopped or minced garlic and 1 teaspoon of crushed red pepper. When sauce is cooked. Remove from skillet. Using same skillet, add the 1/4 cup olive oil and heat. Saute an additional 1 clove of garlic and 1 teaspoon crushed red pepper. When oil is hot, add the spinach and escarole (or endive) a little at a time and cook down, until tender (be careful to not overcook). When greens are cooked. Add tomato mixture and toss with greens. Serve on a salad plate, as an appetizer.

Variation:

For a heartier appetizer, you can add 10-15 medium shrimp, cut in half or Calamari or sgungilli (being careful to not overcook).

Nutrition (per serving): 475 calories

Saturated Fat	3g	
Total Fat	21g	(40% of calories)
Protein	10g	(9% of calories)
Carbohydrates	61g	(52% of calories)
Cholesterol	0mg	
Sodium	402mg	

My Notes and Recipe Variations

Soups, Side Dishes, and Other Tasty Stuff

Grandma's Crab Mustard Sauce

Serves 10

Preparation :05 Cook :00 Stand :15 Total :20

Great for dipping crabs, lobster, fried appetizers or artichokes

Ingredients

1⅓	teaspoons dry mustard
1	cup mayonnaise
2	teaspoons Worcestershire sauce
½	cup heavy or whipping cream
¼	teaspoon salt, Optional

Whip mayonnaise and dry mustard in mixing bowl. While mixing, add Worcestershire sauce and salt. Gradually add in whipping cream until medium firm. Refrigerate for at least 1 hour for better flavor.

Nutrition (per serving): 209 calories

Saturated Fat	6g
Total Fat	23g (98% of calories)
Protein	1g (1% of calories)
Carbohydrates	1g (1% of calories)
Cholesterol	24mg
Sodium	135mg

My Notes and Recipe Variations

Horseradish Sauce

Serves 10

Preparation :10 Cook :00 Stand 1:00 Total 1:10

Great compliment for beef roasts, prime rib, etc...

Ingredients

½	cup white horseradish, finely grated
1½	cups sour cream
2	tablespoons cider vinegar

Finely grate fresh horseradish to yield ½ cup (more is you desire). Blend horseradish, sour cream and vinegar well. Refridgerate overnight for best flavor.

For an extended life, substitute mayonnaise for the sour cream. Refridgerate after making.

Nutrition (per serving): 79 calories

Saturated Fat	3g	
Total Fat	7g	(86% of calories)
Protein	1g	(5% of calories)
Carbohydrates	2g	(9% of calories)
Cholesterol	14mg	
Sodium	15mg	

My Notes and Recipe variations

Grandma Mabel's Bar-B-Que Sauce

(Ribs Tomato Based Barbecue Sauce)

Serves 8

Preparation :15 Cook 1:45 Stand :00 Total 2:00

To get moist and tender ribs, try semi-pressure cooking the spare ribs, then brush the sauce on and finish roasting in oven (basting and turning ribs) or grilling with a pan of water to retain the moisture.

Ingredients

1	12 oz. catsup
1	8 oz. canned tomato sauce
2	teaspoons chili powder
2	teaspoons ground cinnamon
2	dashes hot pepper oil
3	tablespoons balsamic vinegar
1/2	cup water
1/4	cup Worcestershire sauce
4	pounds country-style pork spareribs
2	tablespoons cinnamon
2	tablespoons chili powder
1	teaspoon salt
1	teaspoon black pepper
1	quart water
1/2	cup Worcestershire sauce

In a pressure cooker or large Dutch oven, add 1 quart water, 1/2 cup Worcestershire sauce, 1 teaspoon salt, 1 teaspoon pepper, 2 tablespoons chili powder, 2 teaspoons cinnamon and mix thoroughly. Add to this mixture the ribs. Bring to a boil. Lower heat to low to medium (or if using a pressure cooker to the manufacturers recommendation). Cover and cook for 30-45 minutes.

While the ribs are pre-cooking, prepare the barbecue sauce by add the following ingredients to a saucepan. Catsup, tomato sauce, 2 teaspoons chili power, 2 teaspoons cinnamon, dash of hot pepper oil (more is desired), 3 tablespoons vinegar, 1/2 cup water and 1/4 cup Worcestershire sauce. Mix all the ingredients well and cook over medium heat for 30-45 minutes. Stirring occasionally.

When meat is cooked, remove meat from Dutch oven and place in large roasting pan. Brush both sides of ribs with barbecue sauce. Place pan in 375 degree oven. Baste the ribs with barbecue sauce every 10 minutes, continuously turning and basting the ribs until very tender.

Suggestion:

For barbecue flavor, you can cook the ribs on a grill instead of roasting in the oven. Simply baste and turn the ribs often and make sure that the grill does not get too hot. To prevent grease from splattering, if you have a double rack in your grill, put a pan of water in the lower rack. This will not only catch the drippings, but provide additional moisture so the ribs will not dry out.

Nutrition (per serving): 651 calories

Saturated Fat	12g	
Total Fat	35g	(48% of calories)
Protein	67g	(41% of calories)
Carbohydrates	18g	(11% of calories)
Cholesterol	213mg	
Sodium	1193mg	

My Notes and Recipe Variations

Soups, Side Dishes, and Other Tasty Stuff

Lemon and Dill Dressing

Serves 12

Preparation :10   Cook :00   Stand :15   Total :25

Ingredients

½	cup Dijon mustard
½	teaspoon salt, Optional
1	teaspoon cracked peppercorns
½	cup lemon juice
2	tablespoons dill weed
3	fresh garlic cloves
½	cup white wine vinegar
2	tablespoons sweet onions, finely chopped or minced

Place all ingredients in a blender and mix on high. Store in an airtight container or jar in the refrigerator until ready to use. This is not only a great dressing for salads, but also can be used as a marinade for fish.

Nutrition (per serving): 21 calories

Saturated Fat	0g	
Total Fat	1g	(29% of calories)
Protein	1g	(17% of calories)
Carbohydrates	3g	(54% of calories)
Cholesterol	0mg	
Sodium	253mg	

My Notes and Recipe Variations

Lemon-Mustard Sauce

Serves 10

Preparation :10   Cook :00   Stand :00   Total :10

This sauce is great for using with steamed artichokes or with fish.

Ingredients

1	cup mayonnaise
2 to 4	teaspoons lemon juice, (add a little at a time to obtain the right consistency)
¼	cup Dijon mustard

In a small mixing bowl, add mayonnaise and Dijon mustard. Mix well with a wire whisk, fork or hand blender. Gradually begin adding lemon juice to form a semi-thick sauce. The more lemon juice the looser the consistency. You may wish a looser sauce depending on whether or not the sauce will be used as a dip for artichokes or pouring over seafood.

Nutrition (per serving): 167 calories

Saturated Fat	3g	
Total Fat	18g	(98% of calories)
Protein	0g	(1% of calories)
Carbohydrates	1g	(2% of calories)
Cholesterol	8mg	
Sodium	280mg	

My Notes and Recipe variations

Soups, Side Dishes, and Other Tasty Stuff

Marinara Sauce

Serves 6

Preparation :30 Cook :20 Stand :00 Total :50

Ingredients

2	tablespoons extra light olive oil
4	cloves garlic, minced
1	small onion, diced, chopped
7	pounds Italian tomatoes, (about 2 lbs or fresh, peeled and quarted)
1½	teaspoons salt
1	teaspoon oregano
1	6 oz. tomato paste, (use only if you like a thicker sauce), Optional
1	teaspoon basil, (or 10 fresh basil leaves), Optional
2	tablespoons Italian flat-leaf parsley
¼	cup water, if needed, depending upon liquid from tomatoes

In saucepan or skillet, over medium heat, add olive oil, garlic and onion until tender (3 to 5 minutes). Optionally, add tomato paste and ½ can water (using the tomato paste can). Using a whisk, blend until smooth. Add salt, oregano and stewed tomatoes (and liquid) and break up the tomatoes with a wooden spoon. Stir well making sure all ingredients are mixed together. Lower heat and cook for additional 20-30 minutes. When mixture thickens, it is complete.

Serve over spaghetti, linguine, or other prepared pasta.

Suggestions:

For an added flavorful treat, try adding about 1 pound meaty mushroom (like Porta Bello). Cut into bite sized pieces and saute mushrooms with garlic and onion. Follow the rest of the recipe.

Nutrition (per serving): 178 calories

Saturated Fat	1g
Total Fat	6g (32% of calories)
Protein	5g (11% of calories)
Carbohydrates	26g (58% of calories)
Cholesterol	0mg
Sodium	636mg

My Notes and Recipe variations

Soups, Side Dishes, and Other Tasty Stuff

Vegetable Marinara Sauce

Serves   6

Preparation   :30   Cook   :20   Stand   :00   Total   :50

Ingredients

1	7-inch long yellow squash, sliced and diced
1	7-inch long zucchini, sliced and diced
2	teaspoons extra light olive oil
4	cloves fresh garlic cloves, minced
1	each small onion, diced, chopped
1	28 oz. can canned stewed tomatoes
1	teaspoon salt, Optional
1	teaspoon dried oregano, Optional
1	6 oz. tomato paste
10	black olives, sliced, Optional

Over medium heat, in saucepan or skillet, add olive oil, garlic and onion until tender. Add tomato paste and ½ can water (using the tomato paste can). Using a whisk, blend until smooth.

Add salt, oregano and stewed tomatoes (and liquid). Break up the tomatoes with a wooden spoon. Stir well making sure all ingredients are mixed together. Lower heat and add zucchini and yellow squash. Cook for an addition 20 minutes. When mixture thickens, sauce is complete.

Serve over spaghetti, linguine, or other prepared pasta.

Nutrition (per serving): 95 calories

Saturated Fat	0g
Total Fat	2g (19% of calories)
Protein	3g (13% of calories)
Carbohydrates	16g (68% of calories)
Cholesterol	0mg
Sodium	356mg

My Notes and Recipe Variations

Soups, Side Dishes, and Other Tasty Stuff

Mom Hazel's Barbecue Sauce for Ribs or Chicken

Serves   1

Preparation   :10   Cook   1:00   Stand   :00   Total   1:10

As with any recipe, we all make modifications to old family recipes to suit our tastes. Mom took Grandma Mabel's recipe and made changes for a less sweet variation

Ingredients

3	16 oz. cans tomato sauce
2	Medium sweet onion, diced small
1	stalk celery, finely diced (or ¼ cup celery seed)
1	tablespoon chili powder
½	teaspoon cinnamon Optional
2	tablespoons Worcestershire sauce
2	teaspoons paprika
½	teaspoon black pepper
1	teaspoon salt
¼	teaspoon cloves
2	teaspoons Tabasco sauce
2	tablespoons prepared mustard

Combine all ingredients in a large saucepan, mix well and cook over low heat for 1 hour. Use sauce to brush on meat, then bake in oven or on a barbecue grill. Re-brushing meat every 10 to 15 minutes, during cooking.

Nutrition (per serving): 952 calories for sauce

Saturated Fat	1g
Total Fat	8g (7% of calories)
Protein	34g (14% of calories)
Carbohydrates	186g (78% of calories)
Cholesterol	0mg
Sodium	11921mg

My Notes and Recipe Variations

Mustard Sauce

Serves   6

Preparation   :10   Cook   :00   Stand   1:00   Total   1:10

Great for fish or pork when grilled or baked.

Ingredients

2	tablespoons Dijon mustard
½	teaspoon salt
½	teaspoon pepper
2	teaspoons white wine vinegar
1	teaspoon lemon juice
6	tablespoons vegetable oil, (or cannola)
¼	cup fresh parsley, chopped
½	cup dill, finely chopped

In a blender combine, mustard, salt, pepper, vinegar, lemon juice and oil until mixture is smooth. Stir in the parsley and dill. Place in a sealed container until ready to use. (Refrigerate at least ½ hour so all flavors are fully absorbed).

Nutrition (per serving): 145 calories

Saturated Fat	2g	
Total Fat	14g	(88% of calories)
Protein	1g	(3% of calories)
Carbohydrates	3g	(8% of calories)
Cholesterol	0mg	
Sodium	331mg	

My Notes and Recipe Variations

Marj's Hot Mustard Sauce

Serves   1

Preparation :15 Cook :00 Stand 3:00 Total 3:15

Try this recipe with appetizers, with egg rolls, or as a barbecue sauce for poultry.

Ingredients

4	2 oz. tin Coleman's dry mustard
2	cups sugar
2	oz. bourbon whiskey
2	oz. Jamaican dark rum
2	oz. olive oil
2	oz. tarragon vinegar
4	fresh garlic bulbs, finely chopped or minced
½	cup hot water
1	teaspoon salt

Source: Marj Locke

In a bowl add all ingredients and mix well. Refrigerate for several hours before using or serving.

Nutrition (per serving): 3664 calories

Saturated Fat	14g	
Total Fat	148g	(36% of calories)
Protein	74g	(8% of calories)
Carbohydrates	440g	(48% of calories)
Cholesterol	0mg	
Sodium	2371mg	

My Notes and Recipe variations

Parmesan Peppercorn Dip or Dressing

Serves 20

Preparation :15 Cook :00 Stand :00 Total :15

This dressing/dip is best when chilled overnight to allow all flavors to thoroughly blens.

Ingredients

1	cup sour cream
1	cup plain yogurt
1	cup mayonnaise
2	teaspoons cider vinegar, or lemon juice
$\frac{1}{4}$	cup freshly grated Parmesan cheese
$\frac{1}{4}$	cup Pecorino Romano cheese, finely grated water, or oil, (as needed to thin)
2	teaspoons dry mustard
1	small onion, finely chopped (or $\frac{1}{2}$ teaspoon onion powder)
2	tablespoons cracked peppercorns, (add more if you like a lot of pepper)
2	fresh garlic cloves, finely chopped or minced

Except for the sour cream and yogur, add allingredients in a food processor or blender and mix well on high to ensure full blending.

Add mixture to a bowl and blend in the sour cream and yogurt with a wire wisk until well blended. Place is a dipping bowl

To make a dressing add $\frac{1}{2}$ to 1 cup of milk, blending well. Refridgerate after making.

Nutrition (per serving): 125 calories

Saturated Fat	3g
Total Fat	12g (89% of calories)
Protein	2g (5% of calories)
Carbohydrates	2g (6% of calories)
Cholesterol	12mg
Sodium	104mg

My Notes and Recipe variations

_____
_____
_____
_____
_____
_____
_____
_____
_____
_____
_____
_____
_____
_____
_____
_____
_____
_____

Soups, Side Dishes, and Other Tasty Stuff

Peppers and Onions in Tomato Sauce

Serves   6

Preparation   :10   Cook   :20   Stand   :00   Total   :30

This recipe is great served cold over a pork tenderloin sandwich, hot dogs, bologna or ham. It is also a great side dish served hot with pork or chicken.

Ingredients

4	Italian frying pepper, sweet or hot, quartered
1	large yellow onion
4	green bell peppers, cut into sixths
2	tablespoons extra virgin olive oil
2	teaspoons fresh garlic cloves, minced
1	16 oz. can tomato sauce

salt and pepper, to taste

Clean peppers and cut into pieces about 3x1 in size (quarters, sixths or eighths). Cut onion in half then julienne the halves. Place oil, garlic and onions in a large 12 inch skillet. Saute until onions are tender. Add peppers, stir well and saute an additional 5 minutes. Add the tomato sauce, plus $\frac{1}{2}$ can of water in skillet. Mix well. Cover and let simmer until peppers are al dante. Serve hot as a side dish, over hot dogs, or serve cold with a ham or bologna sandwich, in place of lettuce. If you like a spicier pepper sauce, add crushed red peppers while cooking or hot peppers.

Nutrition (per serving): 122 calories

Saturated Fat	1g	
Total Fat	5g	(36% of calories)
Protein	3g	(9% of calories)
Carbohydrates	17g	(55% of calories)
Cholesterol	0mg	
Sodium	526mg	

My Notes and Recipe variations

Soups, Side Dishes, and Other Tasty Stuff

Aunt Scallie's Spaghetti Sauce

Serves   8

Preparation   :05   Cook   1:30   Stand   :00   Total   1:35

There is nothing better than to try different types of spaghetti sauce with their varying flavors

Ingredients

3	tablespoons olive oil
1/2	medium sweet onion, chopped
3	fresh garlic cloves, cut fine
1	tablespoon fresh parsley, chopped
3	fresh basil leaves
2	bay leaves
1	28 oz. can tomato puree
1	28 oz. can water
1/2	teaspoon baking soda, (to 'kill' acid in tomato sauce)

salt and pepper, to taste

Source: Aunt Scallie

In a 2 to 4 quart (non-aluminum) sauce pan (or Dutch oven), place oil and heat. Add onions, and garlic and saute until tender. Add remaining ingredients and stir well. Cook over a low to medium heat for a minimum of 1½ hours. Serve over pasta, use in Parmigiana recipes.

Nutrition (per serving): 104 calories

Saturated Fat	1g	
Total Fat	5g	(46% of calories)
Protein	2g	(8% of calories)
Carbohydrates	12g	(47% of calories)
Cholesterol	0mg	
Sodium	121mg	

My Notes and Recipe Variations
_____
_____
_____
_____
_____
_____

Spaghetti Sauce with Meat

Serves 15

Preparation :10 Cook 3:00 Stand :00 Total 3:10

Ingredients

1	pound lean ground beef
5	cloves garlic, minced
1	teaspoon salt
1	teaspoon dried oregano
4	28 oz. cans crushed tomato
1	pound pork neck bones, Optional
1	pound beef neck bone, Optional
1	pound beef back ribs, Optional

In Dutch oven or 5 quart pot, saute ground beef. Drain off excess liquid. Add garlic, salt and oregano. Mix well. Add crushed tomatoes and three cans water (using tomato can), and mix well. Bring to boil, then reduce heat to simmer. Add meatballs for 45 minutes. Remove all meat and cook an additional 1 hour, stirring occassionally.

Nutrition (per serving): 2714 calories

Saturated Fat	38g
Total Fat	98g (32% of calories)
Protein	134g (20% of calories)
Carbohydrates	324g (48% of calories)
Cholesterol	340mg
Sodium	3300mg

My Notes and Recipe Variations

Meatless Spaghetti Sauce

Serves 15

Preparation :10   Cook   3:00   Stand   :00   Total   3:10

Ingredients

3   cloves garlic, minced
1   6 oz. can tomato paste
1   28 oz. can tomato puree
3   tablespoons extra light olive oil
1   teaspoon salt
1   teaspoon black pepper
1   teaspoon dried oregano, Optional
1   each bay leaf, Optional

Source: Aunt Jeannie

In a Dutch oven or 5 quart pot, heat oil and saute garlic. Add tomato paste, stir well and saute for 1 minute. Add 3 cans of water (using the tomato paste can). Mix well, heat for 1-2 minutes. Add puree and mix well. Add ½ can of water (using the puree can) and mix well. Add salt and pepper (and oregano and/or bay leaf, optional). Bring to a rapid boil for 15 minutes. Reduce heat and simmer for 2-4 hours, stirring occasionally.

If you wish to add meatballs, add during the last 45 minutes to 1 hour of cooking.

Nutrition (per serving): 62 calories

Saturated Fat	0g	
Total Fat	3g	(42% of calories)
Protein	1g	(9% of calories)
Carbohydrates	8g	(50% of calories)
Cholesterol	0mg	
Sodium	175mg	

My Notes and Recipe Variations

Soups, Side Dishes, and Other Tasty Stuff

Spaghetti Sauce with Anchovies

Serves   6

Preparation   :10   Cook   :45   Stand   :00   Total   :55

Ingredients

2	pounds Italian tomatoes, fresh, peeled and quartered or canned
¼	cup olive oil
2	fresh garlic cloves, thinly sliced
1	2 oz. tin anchovy fillets, chopped
2	tablespoons Italian flat-leaf parsley, chopped
10	oil-cured black olives, pitted and chopped
2	tablespoons tomato paste
¼	cup water

In a large skillet, add oil and heat. Add garlic and saute until tender and lightly browned (very golden). Reduce heat to medium. Add anchovies and black olives. Saute for 5 minutes on medium heat. Add water and tomato paste. Mix well ensuring tomato paste is well blended. Add tomatoes and parsley. Simmer for 30 minutes. Stirring occasionally. Salt and pepper to taste.

Variation:

You can add cubed eggplant, zucchini or broccoli for added flavor and bulk.

Nutrition (per serving): 146 calories

Saturated Fat	2g
Total Fat	11g (65% of calories)
Protein	4g (12% of calories)
Carbohydrates	8g (23% of calories)
Cholesterol	8mg
Sodium	370mg

My Notes and Recipe variations

Soups, Side Dishes, and Other Tasty Stuff

Sauce with Sufretta (Poor Man's Spaghetti Sauce with Meatless 'Meatballs')

Serves   6

Preparation   :30   Cook   1:00   Stand   :00   Total   1:30

Ingredients

Sauce:

2	10 oz. cans tomato paste
6	10 oz. cans water
3	fresh garlic cloves, sliced thin or diced
½	teaspoon salt
½	teaspoon black pepper
2	tablespoons extra light olive oil
1	teaspoon oregano
2	eggs
¼	cup Romano cheese, grated (or Parmesan)
2	teaspoons ready-to-use garlic, chopped
½	teaspoon salt
½	teaspoon black pepper
2	teaspoons dried parsley
2	cups bread crumbs
¼	cup water

Source: Aunt Jeanne

In sauce pan, saute garlic sliced garlic cloves in 2 tablespoons olive oil. Add 2 cans tomato paste and mix. Add 3 cans of water for each can tomato paste, 1 teaspoon oregano. Using a whisk or wooden spoon, mix well. Bring to a boil. Lower heat to medium and cook for 45 minutes to 1 hour.

Sufretta (Poor Man's Meatballs):

Beat 2 eggs, add ¼ cup Romano or Parmesan cheese, ½ cup water, 2 teaspoon chopped garlic, salt, pepper and parsley. Mix well. Gradually add 2 cups of bread crumbs. This will yield about 6 patties or 14 'meatless meatballs'. Shape into patties or balls. In a skillet add a little oil and fry the balls or patties until lightly browned. Add to sauce and cook for 45 minutes.

Nutrition (per serving): 307 calories

Saturated Fat	2g	
Total Fat	10g	(28% of calories)
Protein	11g	(15% of calories)
Carbohydrates	44g	(58% of calories)
Cholesterol	76mg	
Sodium	761mg	

My Notes and Recipe Variations

Aunt Mary Jane's Spaghetti Sauce

Serves   6

Preparation   :10   Cook   1:05   Stand   :00   Total   1:15

Ingredients

1	tablespoon Cannola oil
½	medium sweet onion, chopped fine
½	teaspoon Italian seasoning
3	8 oz. cans tomato sauce, (2 cups)

Source: Auntie Mary Jane

Add Cannola oil to a 2-4 quart saucepan (non aluminum). Heat. Add onions and Italian seasoning. Saute until onions are tender. Add tomato sauce and water. Stir well. Cook for 1-2 hours on medium heat.

Nutrition (per serving): 70 calories

Saturated Fat	0g	
Total Fat	3g	(32% of calories)
Protein	2g	(10% of calories)
Carbohydrates	10g	(58% of calories)
Cholesterol	0mg	
Sodium	687mg	

My Notes and Recipe Variations

Tomato Pesto

Serves 6

Preparation :10   Cook :15   Stand :00   Total :25

Ingredients

60	fresh basil leaves, (or more is desired)
1½	pounds Italian tomatoes, peeled and chopped.
3	fresh garlic cloves, peeled
⅓	cup Italian flat-leaf parsley
1	teaspoon crushed red pepper, (as desired)
⅓	cup extra virgin olive oil
3	tablespoons Pignolli, (or ½ cup walnuts or fresh almonds)

Combine all ingredients, EXCEPT olive oil in food processor and blend on high speed for 1 minute. Slowly add the olive oil. Blend until well mixed. Heat for about 15 minutes, then toss over favorite pasta.

Nutrition (per serving): 168 calories

Saturated Fat	2g
Total Fat	15g (80% of calories)
Protein	2g (4% of calories)
Carbohydrates	7g (17% of calories)
Cholesterol	0mg
Sodium	16mg

My Notes and Recipe Variations

White Clam Sauce

Serves 6

Preparation :20 Cook :10 Stand :00 Total :30

Ingredients

1	6 oz. bottled clam juice
15	large clams, cleaned, shelled, cut, minced
2	cloves fresh garlic cloves, chopped
1/2	cup Italian flat-leaf parsley, chopped
3	tablespoons white wine
1	teaspoon salt
1	bay leaf, crumbled
1	teaspoon dried oregano

In saucepan, add olive oil and garlic. Cook over medium heat until tender. Add clam juice, parsley, wine, salt and bay leaf. Cook for 8-10 minutes. Add clams and bring to a boil. Remove from heat as soon as sauce begins to boil. DO NOT boil the clams. (Cover and keep warm) Sauce will be quite liquid.

Cook pasta slightly underdone. Add clam sauce to drained pasta and let sit for 10 minutes, so pasta can absorb the juice. Serves 4-6 depending on the appetite.

Nutrition (per serving): 47 calories

Saturated Fat	0g	
Total Fat	1g	(11% of calories)
Protein	7g	(58% of calories)
Carbohydrates	2g	(21% of calories)
Cholesterol	18mg	
Sodium	483mg	

My Notes and Recipe Variations

Wine Sauce

Serves   1

Preparation :10   Cook :20   Stand :00   Total :30

Great for any meat or chicken recipe. Use red wine for serving with beef or white wine when serving with chicken.

Ingredients

2	tablespoons butter
2	tablespoons unbleached flour
¼	cup onions, chopped and sauteed
1	cup fresh mushrooms, sliced
¼	cup water
½	cup Riesling or dry white wine, (or dry red wine)

Source: Aunt Jeannie

In medium saucepan, melt butter. Add flour and whip with whisk until smooth. Add sauteed onions, fresh mushroom slices, water and wine. Cook over low to medium heat until mushrooms are tender and sauce slightly thickens. Serve over favorite beef or chicken.

Nutrition (per serving): 383 calories

Saturated Fat	14g
Total Fat	24g (55% of calories)
Protein	4g (4% of calories)
Carbohydrates	20g (20% of calories)
Cholesterol	62mg
Sodium	245mg

My Notes and Recipe Variations

Aunt Helen's Lemon Mustard Dipping Sauce

Serves   10

Preparation   :10   Cook   :00   Stand   :15   Total   :25

Serve with artichokes, fried appetizers and seafood.

Ingredients

1⅓	tablespoons dry mustard
1	cup mayonnaise
2	teaspoons lemon juice
½	cup whipping cream
¼	teaspoon salt, Optional

In mixing bowl combine dry mustard and mayonnaise. Mix well. Add lemon juice (and salt) and continue mixing. Gradually add whipping cream until firm or proper consistency for dipping.

Nutrition (per serving): 209 calories

Saturated Fat	6g	
Total Fat	23g	(97% of calories)
Protein	1g	(1% of calories)
Carbohydrates	1g	(1% of calories)
Cholesterol	24mg	
Sodium	133mg	

My Notes and Recipe variations

Blueberry/Strawberry Sauce (Fruit Sauce)

Serves 8

Preparation :00 Cook :00 Stand :00 Total :00

This fruit sauce is great served hot or cold over cheese blintzes

Ingredients

1   pound fresh strawberry, cleaned
2   tablespoons sugar

Place cleaned strawberries or blueberries in a blender and puree with sugar. Simmer over low heat until sauce begins to thicken. Remove and serve warm over cheese blintze for dessert. If you prefer, make the night before and serve cold over cheese blintze.

Nutrition (per serving): 32 calories

Saturated Fat	0g	
Total Fat	0g	(6% of calories)
Protein	0g	(4% of calories)
Carbohydrates	7g	(90% of calories)
Cholesterol	0mg	
Sodium	1mg	

My Notes and Recipe variations

Cajun Dip/Dressing

Serves 10

Preparation :05 Cook :00 Stand 2:00 Total 2:05

This dip makes for a great spicy flavor. This also can be used as a sauce, served with chicken or shrimp.

Ingredients

¼	cup oil
½	teaspoon garlic powder, (or 1 teaspoon fresh minced garlic)
2	tablespoons lemon juice, fresh
2	teaspoons soy sauce
2	tablespoons green onions, chopped
1	teaspoon coarsely ground black pepper
1	teaspoon celery salt
1	cup mayonnaise, (or 1 cup buttermilk)
1	cup sour cream, (or plain yogurt)
1	teaspoon hot chili powder
1	teaspoon cayenne pepper
3	teaspoons dried onion flakes
1	teaspoon garlic powder
1	teaspoon paprika
2	teaspoons dried parsley
1	dried red hot pepper, finely chopped, grated
1	teaspoon tabasco sauce

Using a blender, mix all ingredients well. Refridgerate overnight for best flavor.

For sauce, add 1 6 oz can of tomato paste and 1-2 cups of water. Mix well and place in saucepan and simmer for 30 minutes. Place chicken or shrimp in a baking pan and add sauce. Bake in 350 degree oven for 35-45 minutes (until chicken or shrimp is cooked).

Nutrition (per serving): 217 calories

Saturated Fat	5g
Total Fat	23g (95% of calories)
Protein	1g (2% of calories)
Carbohydrates	2g (4% of calories)
Cholesterol	17mg
Sodium	142mg

My Notes and Recipe Variations

Soups, Side Dishes, and Other Tasty Stuff

Serves   8

Preparation   :10   Cook   :00   Stand   :15   Total   :25

This is a very basic recipe for blending the two cheeses together. The possibilites are endless for different flavors for dips. See recommendations

Ingredients

1	cup cream cheese
1	cup sour cream
1	teaspoon milk, (more may be used, if needed for proper consistency)

Soften cream cheese to room temperature. Add sour cream and milk. Mix well. To cream cheese mixture, add any of the following ingredients. If you use dried ingredients, liquid will have to slowly be increased, since the dried ingredients will absorb the liquid.

1. Add 1 tablespoon finely diced onion or scallion (or use dried minced onion and increase liquid)

2. Add 2 finely chopped garlic cloves (or 1 or 2 teaspoons of garlic powder)

3. Mix onion and garlic for a great chip dip

4. Add 1 teaspoon minced onion, 2 sun dried tomatoes, ¼ teaspoon parsley, ¼ teaspoon garlic powder

5. ½ teaspoon garlic powder, ½ teaspoon chili powder, ½ teaspoon cayenne pepper

6. 2 tablespoons fresh finely chopped carrots, 1 finely chopped celery stalk, ½ teaspoon ground pepper corns

7. Don't limit yourself

Nutrition (per serving): 166 calories

Saturated Fat	8g
Total Fat	16g (88% of calories)
Protein	3g (7% of calories)
Carbohydrates	2g (5% of calories)
Cholesterol	43mg
Sodium	96mg

My Notes and Recipe variations

Soups, Side Dishes, and Other Tasty Stuff

Gorgonzola Cheese Sauce

Serves   8

Preparation   :00   Cook   :00   Stand   :00   Total   :00

Gorgonzola cheese is made in Gorgonzola Italy a small town in Lombardy, 11 miles northeast of Milan ~ heart of cheese producing country

Ingredients

¼	cup unbleached flour
1	cup gorgonzola cheese, crumbled
3	cups milk

In a large saucepan, add the butter and flour and stir with a whisk over a low to medium heat to create a roux (paste made by heating butter and flour). Once the roux is well mixed, gradually add the milk, continuosly whisking the sauce. Simmer the mixture for approximately 30 minutes. Crumble the Gorgonzola cheese and slowly stir into the milk mixture. Continue stirring until the sauce is smooth. Continue simmering for another 15-20 minutes over a low heat until the sauce is thick and smooth. Add salt and pepper to taste

Nutrition (per serving): 135 calories

Saturated Fat	5g	
Total Fat	8g	(55% of calories)
Protein	6g	(22% of calories)
Carbohydrates	8g	(23% of calories)
Cholesterol	25mg	
Sodium	283mg	

My Notes and Recipe variations

Yellow Pepper Pesto

Serves 6

Preparation :15 Cook :00 Stand :00 Total :15

Ingredients

15	yellow bell peppers, large, cleaned and quartered (15-20 peppers)
3	tablespoons PIGNOLLi, (pine nuts)
3	fresh garlic cloves
¼	cup Pecorino Romano cheese
¼	teaspoon crushed red pepper
1	cup extra virgin olive oil, (minus 2 tablespoons)

In a food processor, add all ingredients EXCEPT oil. Blend or chop and mix well. On high speed, SLOWLY add the oil, until mixture is well blended and smooth. Place in saucepan and gently heat. Serve over pasta.

Another great recipe to serve over medium sized pasta or ravioli.

Nutrition (per serving): 424 calories

Saturated Fat	6g	
Total Fat	40g	(84% of calories)
Protein	3g	(3% of calories)
Carbohydrates	13g	(13% of calories)
Cholesterol	3mg	
Sodium	47mg	

My Notes and Recipe Variations

Calzone	344
Capellini Pomodoro	150
Capellini w/Calamari	84
Cavatelle	152

Chicken

Bracioli	96
Breaded Chicken	24
Cacciatore	30
Chicken Paprika	42
Cornish Hen w/Wild Rice Stuffing	58
Florentine	60
Fra Diavlo	32
Fried	62
Garlic	50
Italiano	36
Kabob	56
Lemon Wine Sauce	40
Mediterranean	38
Onions and Peppers	52
Oregano	54

Parmigiana	44
Pomodoro	46
Prosciutto	26
Rice Florentine	28
Spicy in Tomatoe Sauce	32
Spicy, in Tomatoe Sauce	32
Wine Sauce	34
Wings, Hot & Spicy	48
Italian Style	306
w/Noodles	304
Cream of Chicken	310

Cole Slaw	216
Corn Salad	203
Cornish Hen w/Wild Rice Stuffing	58
Cucumber Salad, Vinegar & Dill	207
Dill Potato Salad	208

Dipping Sauce

Cajun	404

Pasta

Pork

Potato

Tomatoe w/Onion	390
White Clam Sauce	400
Yellow Pepper Pesto	409
Spare Ribs, Braised	98
Spinach & Beans	274
Spinacio y Figiuolo	274
Squash Medley	276
Steak, Mushroom & Wine Sauce	116
String Beans, Pork Flavored	261
Stuffed Peppers	350
Stuffed Shells, Filling	176
Wine Sauce for Beef or Chicken	401
Sauerbraten	112
Sausage & Peppers	114

Seafood

Calamari w/Capellini84	
Calamari, Fried	82
Calamari, Stuffed in Tomato Sauce	88
Pasta Primavera	70

Shrimp Italiano	86
Shrimp Scampi	83
Shrimp, Breaded	80
Short Ribs, Braised	98
Shrimp Italiano	86
Shrimp Scampi	83
Shrimp, Breaded	80

Side Dish
Rice

Wild Rice Stuffing	352
Arborio w/Mushroom	292
Arborio w/Onion and Herbs	296
Fried	288
Spanish Style	294
Vegetables & Cheese	290

Soup

Barszcz	298
Beet & Chicken	298
Broccoli, Cream of	308

Recipe	Page #	Recipe	Page #

My Recipe - Quick Finder

Recipe	Page #	Recipe	Page #

Recipe	Page #	Recipe	Page #

My Recipe - Quick Finder

Recipe	Page #	Recipe	Page #

Recipe Consideration Form
(mail recipes to: From the Hearth, Recipe Consideration, PO Box 2368, Darien, IL 60561

(Please PRINT)
Name of contributor: _____   Recipe from: _____
            (Please print)
(Self, which relative, name of relative)
Address: _____
Phone Number: _____   Fax: _____   E-Mail: _____
Name of Recipe: _____   When Recipe Used: _____
                                            (holidays, birthdays, etc...)

Ingredients
_____   _____   _____
_____   _____   _____
_____   _____   _____
_____   _____   _____

Preparation Time: _____   Cooking Time: _____   Setting Time: _____
Instructions:
_____
_____
_____
_____
_____

Instructions (con't)

_____
_____
_____
_____

My Fond Memories:

_____
_____
_____
_____

Disclaimer

This disclaimer must be signed in order to be considered for publication in the From the Hearth - World Wide Collection.

By signing below, I certify that the recipe submitted to From the Hearth for consideration of inclusion in the World Wide Collection Book, is an authentic family/friend recipe, to the best of my knowledge and has not been copied from any published publication. This statement releases the owner, publisher, printers and other associates of From the Hearth or KMS Publishing, Inc from any liability of false misrepresentation of said recipe.

Print Name: _____ Signature: _____ Date: _____

Order Form

To order additional Copies of *From the Hearth vol 1*, or to order copies for gifts, please fill in the information below. (You may photocopy this form) Mail Orders to: KMSPublishing, PO Box 2368, Darien, IL 60561

Qty x Cost = total

___$24.95 = _____ From the Hearth - Volume I (Polish, Italian, European and American Recipes)

Total= _____

P&H= _____ (Postage & Handling, add $3.95 for 1 book, $6.75 for 2 books, $9.00 for 3 books. Add $2.75 for each additional book ordered over 3 copies.

Total Remitted= _____

Wholesale orders or Non-for-Profit Organizations wishing to sell this cookbook, please write to above address or E-Mail us at www.info@fromthehearth.com

Pay Method: Check _____ Money Order _____ Amex _____ VI _____ MC _____ DI _____

Please Print the Following Information:

Credit Card No: _____   Exp Date: _____

Billing Name: _____   Ship To Name: _____

Billing Address: _____   Shipping Address: _____

Billing Address: _____   Shipping Address: _____

City/State/Zip _____   City/State/Zip: _____

Phone # _____   Phone # _____

E-Mail Address: _____

Signature Required: _____   Date of Order: _____

Order Form

To order additional Copies of *From the Hearth vol 1*, or to order copies for gifts, please fill in the information below. (You may photocopy this form) Mail Orders to: KMSPublishing, PO Box 2368, Darien, IL 60561

Qty x Cost = total

___$24.95 = _____ From the Hearth - Volume I (Polish, Italian, European and American Recipes)

Total=   _____

P&H=   _____ (Postage & Handling, add $3.95 for 1 book, $6.75 for 2 books, $9.00 for 3 books. Add $2.75 for each additional book ordered over 3 copies.

Total Remitted= _____

Wholesale orders or Non-for-Profit Organizations wishing to sell this cookbook, please write to above address or E-Mail us at www.info@fromthehearth.com

Pay Method: Check _____   Money Order_____   Amex _____   VI _____   MC_____   DI _____

Please Print the Following Information:

Credit Card No: _____   Exp Date: _____

Billing Name: _____   Ship To Name: _____

Billing Address: _____   Shipping Address: _____

Billing Address: _____   Shipping Address: _____

City/State/Zip _____   City/State/Zip: _____

Phone # _____   Phone # _____

E-Mail Address: _____

Signature Required: _____   Date of Order: _____

Baked Sweet Potato

Serves   8

Preparation   :15   Cook   1:40   Stand   :00   Total   1:55

Ingredients

8 to 10	sweet potatoes, or yams
1$^1/_2$	sticks butter
2	tablespoons butter
$^1/_2$	cup brown sugar
2	tablespoons flour
$^1/_2$	teaspoon cinnamon, or cardamon
4	tablespoons walnuts, chopped (or pecans)
1	apple, sliced and peeled

Source: Merlo Bailey

Clean and peel potatoes. Cut into bite sized pieces. Place potatoes in 5 quart pot and cover with water. Bring to a boil and cook until potatoes are tender. Drain potatoes (reserving liquid, if desired, for gravy). Return potatoes to pot, add 1$^1/_2$ sticks butter and mash. Place in a casserole dish.

In a separate bowl, add 2 tablespoons butter, softened, $^1/_2$ cup brown sugar, 2 tablespoons flour, cinnamon or cardamon. Cut into butter. Stir in nuts. Sprinkle half of the mixture over potatoes and sprinkle with remaining topping. Bake for 35-40 minutes in a 350 degree oven.

Brussel Sprouts Italiano

Serves   4

Preparation :10   Cook :45   Stand :00   Total :55

Ingredients

1	pound brussels sprouts, trimmed and washed
4 to 6	cups boiling water
2	fresh garlic cloves, peeled and smashed
2	tablespoons fresh lemon juice
$1/4$	cup Romano cheese

salt and pepper, to taste

Bring water to a boil in a 2 to 4 quart saucepan. Add brussel sprouts and cook until outer area is tender, but center is still a little under cooked. While brussel sprouts are cooking, add olive oil to a medium skillet and heat. Add garlic and saute until browned. Remove garlic and cool. Chop up and add brussel sprouts in 2nd step, if desired.

When Brussel sprouts are done, drain well and add to the oil in the skillet. Season with salt and pepper. Stir carefully and cook for several minutes (about 3 minutes). Add lemon juice and cook for 2-3 more minutes. Remove from skillet and place in a heated serving dish and sprinkle with Romano cheese. Serve immediately.

Variation:

Instead of the Romano cheese, using same skillet, add 2 tablespoons of butter. and $1/4$ to $1/2$ cup of seasoned bread crumbs. Heat and mix well, forming a crumbly mixture. Spoon over Brussel sprouts and serve.

Double Baked Sweet Potatoes

Serves   4

Preparation :00 Cook :00 Stand :00 Total :00

Ingredients

2   large sweet potatoes
1   egg
2   tablespoons butter
2   tablespoons cream
brown sugar, to sprinkle on top, Optional

Clean sweet potatoes. Bake sweet potatoes in a 350 to 375 degree oven for 45 minutes to 1 hour, until done. Remove from oven. Cut potatoes in half and scoop out the potato from the skin (retain skin). Put potato pulp in a blender and add butter, cream and egg. Whip until light. Divide the potato mixture and spoon into skins. Top with brown sugar, if desired. Return to oven and bake an additional 10 minutes until the tops are golden brown and the potato is heated thoroughly. Serve with ham steak or other pork dish.

Nutrition (per serving): 195 calories

Saturated Fat	5g	
Total Fat	9g	(42% of calories)
Protein	3g	(7% of calories)
Carbohydrates	25g	(51% of calories)
Cholesterol	75mg	
Sodium	90mg	

My Notes and Recipe variations

Eggplant Parmigiana

Serves   6

Preparation :15   Cook 2:30   Stand :00   Total   2:45

A favorite as a meal or a hearty side dish. Italian eggplants are much smaller and less bitter than regular eggplant, although you can use the larger American eggplant (just reduce the quantity, since they are 2 to 3 times larger).

Ingredients

SPAGHETTI SAUCE - MEATLESS

8	Italian eggplants, cleaned and sliced to $\frac{1}{4}$"
$\frac{1}{2}$	cup unbleached flour
1	large egg
2	tablespoons water
2	cups mozzarella cheese, shredded
$\frac{1}{2}$	cup Romano cheese, grated

Make the meatless spaghetti sauce. Wash eggplants and remove ends. There is an ongoing debate as to whether or not to peel the skin. (I don't peel the skin, since the frying of the eggplant, makes the skin tender.) Slice the eggplant to $\frac{1}{4}$ inch sliced. In a medium bowl, beat egg with water. In a large skillet, add 2-3 tablespoons olive or cannola oil. Heat. Dip eggplant in egg mixture, then into flour. Place in heated skillet. Fry eggplant (on medium heat) on both sides until light golden brown and tender.

Remove from oil and place on paper towels to drain. Repeat process until all eggplant is cooked. In a large baking dish (15x11x2), place some spaghetti sauce in bottom to cover. Place one layer of eggplant over sauce. (For added flavor, sprinkle Romano cheese lightly over eggplant). Cover with mozzarella, then top with more sauce. Add a second layer of eggplant, cheese and sauce. Bake in a 350 degree oven for $1\frac{1}{2}$-2 hours, until eggplant is medium soft and cheese is lightly browned. Serve with extra sauce and Romano cheese.

Escarole y Figuolo (Escarole and White Beans)

Serves   6

Preparation   :10   Cook   :30   Stand   :00   Total   :40

Even as a kid, this was one of my favorite vegetables.

Ingredients

2	bunches escarole, (fresh, torn into small pieces)
4	cups boiling water, (about ¼ of depth of escarole)
½ to 1	teaspoon sea salt
4	fresh garlic cloves, chopped fine
116	oz. can white beans,(we prefer Northern White beans)

Source: Aunt Scallie

Clean the escarole well under cool running water. Tear into small pieces. Using a 4 quart saucepan, place water in pan (about ¼ full) and add salt. Bring to a boil. Add escarole and cook until tender (not soft).

Drain the escarole, using a colander and reserve part of the liquid. In a large skillet, add oil and heat. Add garlic and saute until tender and lightly browned. Add drained escarole and beans (you can add the entire can of beans or drain and rinse the beans before using), stir well and saute until beans and escarole are hot.

Serve with Italian or French bread. Makes a delicious meal or side dish.

Mixed Fried Vegetables - Italian Style

Serves   6

Preparation   :10   Cook   2:00   Stand   :00   Total   2:10

Ingredients

2	7-inch long eggplants, (use Italian eggplants) cut into julienne slices or sticks
1	cup unbleached flour
3 to 4	tablespoons extra virgin olive oil
¾	cup warm water
1	egg white, lightly beaten
2	zucchini, julienned, cut into strips
½	teaspoon oregano
1	tablespoon Romano cheese, grated
2	yellow squash, julienned

oil, for frying

salt, to taste

Cut eggplant in half and then lengthwise into 3 inch sticks. Cut zucchini and squash into sticks..

Place flour, oregano, Romano cheese, and salt, to taste, in a bowl. Add olive oil and water and stir until smooth. Set aside for several hours. In a deep fryer or large skillet, heat about ½ to ¾ inch of oil. Beat egg white until soft peaks form and fold into batter until blended. Dip vegetables and cheese, if desired, into the batter and fry in hot oil until browned. Drain on a paper towel.

Nutrition (per serving): 386 calories

Saturated Fat	1g
Total Fat	4g (8% of calories)
Protein	13g (13% of calories)
Carbohydrates	76g (78% of calories)
Cholesterol	5mg
Sodium	120mg

My Notes and Recipe Variations

Salads and Vegetables

Pepperoni Fritti

Serves   6

Preparation   :10   Cook   :15   Stand   :00   Total   :25

Serve with beef for beef sandwiches, or use in place of mayonnaise and lettuce in a sandwich.

Ingredients

8	large green bell peppers, cored and cut into 1 inch strips
½	cup olive oil
2 to 4	fresh garlic cloves

salt and pepper, to taste

Wash peppers and remove stems and cores. Rinse well. Slice into 1 inch strips. Let drain, then dry on paper towels to remove excess water. Heat oil in a large skillet. Add peppers and garlic. Fry over medium heat, turning frequently. (You may also wish to add some onions). Add salt and pepper to taste. Fry (or saute) until peppers are tender or tender crisp and cooked. Serve with beef.

Nutrition (per serving): 205 calories

Saturated Fat	2g	
Total Fat	18g	(80% of calories)
Protein	1g	(2% of calories)
Carbohydrates	9g	(17% of calories)
Cholesterol	0mg	
Sodium	67mg	

My Notes and Recipe Variations

Potatoes-Baked

Serves   4

Preparation   :10   Cook   1:00   Stand   :00   Total   1:10

Ingredients

4   baking potatoes
4   tablespoons olive oil
4   fresh garlic cloves, minced
4   tablespoons chives, chopped
1   teaspoon salt
pepper, to taste

Wash skins of the potatoes. Cut a slice into the potatoes (about ¼") either across the long or short end. DO NOT cut all the way through. In a small saute pan, add the olive oil and garlic.

Saute until the garlic is tender and the oil has absorbed the flavor. (several minutes). Add the chopped chives (or scallions) and mix well. Spoon the oil, garlic and onion-chive mixture evenly over all of the potatoes, trying to drip the oil between each slice.

Place on a baking sheet and bake in a 425 to 450 degree oven for 1 hour (until potatoes are tender) and tops are lightly browned.

You can use any combination of fresh herbs to add more flavor to this easy to make recipe.

Pierogi-Cheese Filling (Polish Style Pasta)

Serves 30

Preparation :05 Cook :05 Stand :00 Total :10

Ingredients

1	cup dry curd cottage cheese
1	egg yolk, beaten
1	teaspoon sugar
1	teaspoon butter
1/2	teaspoon onions, grated

salt, to taste

Source: Gloria Kuska

   Beat all ingredients in a bowl until smooth. Spoon into Pierogi dough and cook as directed.

Nutrition (per serving): 7 calories

Saturated Fat	0g
Total Fat	0g (38% of calories)
Protein	1g (49% of calories)
Carbohydrates	0g (13% of calories)
Cholesterol	8mg
Sodium	15mg

My Notes and Recipe variations

Serves   6

Preparation   :30   Cook   :45   Stand   :00   Total   1:15

Ingredients

4	large potatoes
1/2	cup milk
1	egg
1	egg yolk
1/2	pound unbleached flour

Peel and cube potatoes. Place in pot of salted water and boil until tender. Using a rice masher, mash the potatoes (or grate).

In large bowl, add potatoes and mix well with milk until moist. Blend 1 egg and 1 yolk. Mix well. Gradually add milk until dough is light. Add more milk or melted butter as necessary, to make dough light and fluffy. This dough can be used as a dumpling and placed into hot liquid or soup stock or can be rolled into ⅛ inch thick dough and cut with a 4 inch pastry/cookie cutter and stuffed with plums, blueberries, sauerkraut, etc. Use one of the Pierogi filling recipes to fill.

Serves   6

Preparation :10   Cook :20   Stand :00   Total :30

Ingredients

Make PIEROGI DOUGH #1, as directed
2	cups canned plums, (reserve the plum juice)
¼	cup water
2	tablespoons sugar, Optional
2	teaspoons lemon juice, (fresh squeezed is preferred)
2 to 3	tablespoons butter

Make Pierogi dough as directed and cut out appropriate shapes. (The dough circles may need to be larger than 4 inches try 5-6 inches). Drain plums, remove pit, and reserve liquid. Place one plum in the center of the Pierogi shape. Fold over dough to meet ends and crimp. Cook Pierogi in a pot of simmering water (no salt). Until done (about 5-8 minutes). Remove Pierogi's and drain.

In a large skillet, melt the butter. Add the plum juice with ¼ cup water and 2 teaspoons lemon juice and sugar until it slightly thickens. Add the Pierogi to the mixture and saute on both sides until well heated. Place the plums in a serving bowl and pour remaining syrup over them. Serve as a dessert.

You may use other stewed fruits, such as apricots in place of the plums.

Variation:

You can use Fresh plums, instead of canned, like my Auntie Anna use to make.
10-12	large sweet plums; pitted
½	cup sugar
2	cups water

In a saucepan, add plums, sugar and water. Bring to a boil and

Pierogi-Mashed Potato and Sauerkraut

(Kartofle Puree y Kiszona Kapusta Filling for)

Serves 10

Preparation :15   Cook :45   Stand :00   Total 1:00

Pierogi's can be stuffed with almost anything. You can also use the Sauerkraut recipe in the book, instead of the sauerkraut listed.

Ingredients

Prepare PIEROGI DOUGH # 1 as directed
4   large potatoes, cooked and mashed
1   16 oz. jar Frank's Polish Style Sauerkraut
1   tablespoon butter
1   small onion, finely diced

   Clean and peel potatoes. Cut into bite sized pieces. Boil and cook until tender. Drain well and mash with 1 tablespoon butter. In small skillet, saute 1 tablespoon butter and diced onion, until tender. Add sauerkraut and mix well. Spoon into Pierogi dough and cook as directed.

Nutrition (per serving): 194 calories

Saturated Fat	1g
Total Fat	2g (12% of calories)
Protein	5g (9% of calories)
Carbohydrates	38g (79% of calories)
Cholesterol	12mg
Sodium	455mg

My Notes and Recipe Variations

Pierogi-Sauerkraut Filling

Serves 30

Preparation :10   Cook :15   Stand :00   Total :25

Slight variation to the Sauerkraut filling

Ingredients

4	28 oz. cans sauerkraut
2 to 3	tablespoons oil
1	small onion
1	tablespoon salt
½	teaspoon pepper, to taste

Source: Gloria Kuska

Drain sauerkraut (for a less sour sauerkraut, rinse the cabbage under running water). In a 4 quart Dutch oven or pot, place the drained sauerkraut and fill with water until the 'kraut' is covered. Cover the pot. Cook for 35-40 minutes. Drain the sauerkraut and cool to room temperature. Squeeze out water from sauerkraut and place on a cutting board and chop.

Place oil in a skillet (preferably cast iron), or use an electric skillet set to 400 degrees. Heat skillet and oil. Add chopped onions and brown. Add 1 tablespoon salt, sauerkraut and sprinkle with pepper. Mix well. Continue to cook (fry) the sauerkraut. Pour a little more oil on the top of the sauerkraut. Turn over the sauerkraut and continue frying until all is lightly browned.

Cool to room temperature before using as filling.

Pierogi-Sweet Cheese Filling

Serves 10

Preparation :15 Cook :15 Stand :30 Total 1:00

This makes a tasty dessert, or sweet side dish to pork or chicken recipes. These cheese filled Pierogi's are great served with the plum Pierogi's and plum sauce, rather than butter. Sour cream also adds a nice addition for a topping.

Ingredients

1	pound cottage cheese, large curd (dry is better)
2	tablespoons sugar, (for a sweeter filling add 1-2 tablespoons more)
1	egg yolk
$\frac{1}{2}$	teaspoon salt
1	cup sour cream
4	tablespoons butter, melted and hot.

Using a sieve (or strainer) sieve the cheese (push through strainer using the back of a spoon) into a bowl. Beat in the sugar, egg yolk, 1 tablespoon cooled melted butter and 1 cup sour cream ($\frac{1}{4}$ cup at a time). Beat well until thoroughly mixed.

Spoon filling into Pierogi dough, crimp and seal. Let Pierogi stand for about $\frac{1}{2}$ hour. Bring a large pot of water to a boil, then reduce to a simmer. Cook the Pierogi for 8-10 minutes until they float to surface. Remove and transfer to a heated plate. Serve warm with melted butter and bread crumb mixture over the top.

Pierogi Dough-1 (Ciasto Pierogi)

Serves   6

Prep   1:00   Cook   :30   Stand   :00   Total   1:30

There are different variations to the Pierogi dough. This is just one way to make it.

Ingredients

2   cups unbleached flour
1   tablespoon butter, melted
½   teaspoon salt
2   eggs
water, as needed

Place flour in medium mixing bowl. Add melted butter, salt and eggs. Mix well. Gradually add a little water at a time (about 1 tablespoon at a time). Mixing between water addition, until soft dough is formed.

Turn out onto a lightly floured surface and roll into a large rectangle about ⅛ inch thick. Using a 4 inch circular cookie/dough cutter, cut the dough into as many PIEROGI shapes as possible.

Spoon whatever filling you desire into center of dough. Fold over dough pieces so that edges meet. Lightly brush the inside edges with egg whites to help adhere the dough better. Crimp ends using your thumb or the tines of a fork. To cook Pierogi, place in simmering salted water for about 5 minutes. Remove when done and place on paper towel to remove excess water. For non-fruit Pierogi's, after you remove from water, place some butter in a skillet and melt. Add Pierogi and cook for 2-3 minutes, until golden. Remove from skillet. Add bread crumbs to remaining butter in skillet and saute. Spoon bread crumb mixture over Pierogi. Serve hot.

Fillings:
   1. Sauerkraut 2. Plums 3. Blueberries 4. Mashed potatoes